Our Story Begins

Alexander G. Valdez

Our Story Begins
By Alexander Valdez
ISBN: 978-0-9848220-2-7
LCCN: 2012952462

Published by Vision Quest Entertainment Incorporated
Salem, Oregon

Do you have a Question, Comment, or Complaint about this publication? Help us improve our product by giving your insights at our company website:
www.visionquestentertainmentincorporated.com

Zen Circle Design based on an Enso by EUN (1598-1679), the 184th abbot of Daitokuji Monastery.

The Shaman Logo is protective. The Shaman Logo functions as an open brand with closed intent. These ideas are protected. Actual Emulation should not go beyond use in creative writing or homage.

This book is a bias-based book and undergoing vetting. I am accepting fine criteria. The Army vetting for this book, "Our Story Begins" and the other two books in the Project Period Series: "The Writer's Guide to the Hero's Journey" and "Screenwriter's Notebook: A Remedial Step-by-Step Guide to Finishing Your Screenplay" are paid for by the $5 owed me from Space Invaders. I anticipate an ARMY LOGO on all of these books for the effort and accuracy. I also expect this book will be a Justice Department Book as paid for by the material

presented in the second chapter. The main copy is the spiral bound version, which contains handbook and draft, lengthy biography and endnotes. More copies of this paperback book are available for vetting at www.createspace.com/3892886
Academic edition https://www.createspace.com/4014556
Hardcover version http://www.lulu.com/content/hardcover-book/our-story-begins/13255913

ACKNOWLEDGMENTS

This book is written with my memory of "FineLine" Frank Barnes, whom I apprenticed under and who taught me who a master contractor can be. When I had set forth after being your apprentice, you had proven yourself a painter for seven years, an apprentice for seventeen years and a master contractor for life. You said, "People exist who are wrongful powerful. I can still be right filled." On contracts and life, thank you for your giving.

TABLE OF CONTENTS

This book is openly bias-based, and I accept a bias-based tradition.[1]

---

[1] If the length of the footnotes has offended more than a page, then to the end, without regret, I have placed these acknowledgements in the back.

DEDICATION

This book is dedicated to people who like to tell stories, and who like to imagine and believe. Be straightforward in your truth; do not be afraid of your results. As for heading and heeding, live exceptionally and be well.

Love Always,

Alexander Valdez

LEARNING FROM THE CINEMA-LIBRE

I consider the Cinema-Libre an expression of religion for me, although a part of my religion and, a part which anyone can participate in without me being heavy-handed or overly proselytizing. I still consider the films' approachability by other people who have different religious upbringings highly important, endeavoring towards a cinema where they can maintain their uniqueness and gifts and we may all grow.

The movement is guided by tenets that are meant to improve us and I understand we benefit ourselves and others to establish thoughts worth having into our heads, and also our cinematagraphígue[2].

---

[2] I have had the opportunity to spend time amongst many religions of the world, including their children. What I would want for the children of the world is for them to feel, "You don't have to be the best at everything but I would like you to feel respected for what you have chosen to do."

I am working towards building a feeling cinema, guided by the things that make us human and humane, provoking to inclusion and honesty. I wish to feature characters driven to decisions, which represent humanity, and that which is primitive to primate and complex to words.

I have three tenets to point the way. I feel, in my tenets, the second tenet[3] is the most approachable for an audience who is interested in a shared intellectual discourse, including and involving what the characters in the narrative struggle with on the screen. My second tenet deals with the following diverse concepts:

MEDITATION

Be Mindful and conscious. Concentrate on breathing in and breathing out. Allow thoughts of a conflictual nature to simply pass. Control your thoughts and allow yourself to be the source mind of origin. Think deliberately.

Meditations may be formal or informal. An example of a formal meditation is Vipassana Meditation, which the

---

[3] The second tenet states: All films created under the Cinema-Libre Code must be as positive as possible in nature, with the heroes representing loving-kindness and the beauty, truth, and difficulty natural to the state of the human condition. They should further teach tested and real techniques to the audience for the liberation from worldly suffering, as best understood by the filmmakers, including: meditation, presence, communion, forgiveness, sobriety, surrender, self-actualization and finding inner peace, calm, and joy.

Theravada[4] have stated I may share my version of in this text: Most thoughts in your head occur as an event with you as the source mind of origin. Others manifest from others, they have said something, or done something, or led you to believe something. Breathing in and Breathing out, allow these thoughts to pass. If you observe your thoughts, note them only to be leaving while breathing in and breathing out. Give yourself a half an hour, probably seated comfortably, and focus on your breathing.

PRESENCE

Be Here Now. The future is an expectation, the past is already done. Be in the eternal now, and know even in the past, this was the now of the then. Even in the future, you will be in the now of the then. Allow others to partake of you in this moment, honestly. Experience as fully that which in the now is real and untroubling to you and know you have no other moment but the eternal now to improve your current situation. Work, in the now, to your best contentment. Breath. Allow thoughts which are not yours to pass from your mind, and allow that which you would put

---

[4] More information about the Theravada is available in their book, Handbook for Mankind.

forward in yourself to be what is the feeling and thinking you experience.

COMMUNION

More than one person can share in success. More than one person can feel successful in an endeavor.   In Christianity, we share an observation called Formal Communion.   I was once an Acolyte in the Evangelical Lutheran Church and I am still legally able to hold towel at baptism and to provide wafer and substance for communion. As an acolyte, my duty is to carry the flame of faith and to make sure the snuffer snuffs the candle at the end.

Communion, in Christianity, is a formal-process that allows all people to share in forgiveness and acceptance due to Christ's sacrifice and share amongst other Christians our acceptance of them as a whole-person. Christ on the cross has earned this and we now partake of what is owed, when after his lashes he was blameless and sinless in the laws of man and eyes of God, yet still crucified. In this observance-ceremony of Christian-Communion, we forgive each other for the human we are, and allow God room for forgiveness.

Another example I do not doubt, and I have had the pleasure of participating in, is bowing down with other Muslims in prayer and observance. As I stated, more than one can share in success. In my Buddhist studies, the people who hear the monk speak bring food and supplies for the week. After hearing the monk speak, the attendees line up in a semi-circle and share in holding the rice they or others brought to put at least a spoonful of rice in each of the monks' begging bowls. For the Theravada, they return to the table and give the now ample rice back to those who gave the rice to them. They then bless all of the food and say "Sato." All in attendance, monk and attendee both, share in the food, diverse and nutritious, a feast for those days of congregation at least, and meant to last the monks for the week. All three examples are a beautiful communion, and integral to their religion.

FORGIVENESS

The benefit of forgiveness is the forgiver is no longer burdened by emotion. This feeling of no longer being burdened is often true of people given forgiveness, as well. Christianity is often rightfully associated with the concept of forgiveness.[5] Even non-Christian religions recognize

---

[5] Martin Luther, German Theologians and major figure founder of the Protestant Reformation, felt four types of forgiveness can be defined: 1) Being told by God things are allowed for oneself, even if not allowed others, before or after the act of committing them. 2) Being told of things God insists to be done ahead of time by God which will be done and do not anger him. 3) Seeking forgiveness from

forgiveness functions in two basic patterns: one is outward, the other inward. I feel worth mention, self-forgiveness to the similar qualities listed in the footnote. Forgiveness of oneself is often intrinsic to the artist, and necessary for powerful, vulnerable art.

Forgiveness means both to emote and to not be sabotaged by emotion. Get past the mess, get past the chaos. Create: Imperfect Works. Be Prolific.

Much of Buddhism is intellectual, "I don't want to suffer anymore." A Good Buddhist would endeavor to the eight-fold path of Right-View, Right-Intention, Right-Speech, Right-Action, Right-Livelihood, Right-Effort, Right-Mindfulness, and Right-Concentration to avoid the need for forgiveness.[6]

Christianity recognizes human failure. Christians offer the heartfelt, "I want this suffering over." Both paths to non-suffering, Buddhist and Christian, are actionable and admirable well-practiced.

God due to guilt or shame. 4) Forgiveness granted to us by Christ's sacrifice on the cross. Martin Luther also mentioned forgiveness of others.

[6] Also, to the first two Forgiveness patterns in the Martin Luther example, previously, these Buddhist guidelines are given ahead of time.

SOBRIETY

I emulate our current President Barack Obama in honesty. I have, in my life, used alcohol, tobacco, marijuana (even medically), cocaine, methamphetamine, PCP (Supplied by the Army for drug resistance training), Sodium Pentothal (same) and I have even smoked opium once by mistake in college at Bluesfest in Chicago and later, heroin when my marijuana pipe was spiked without my knowledge in a very social situation where I was alone with a group of young women. I have not used them addictively and I actively avoid addiction. I do not like chemical drugs, myself. The closer to a plant grown from seed the better. I shun anything where I know people lose control. I feel better about myself. I clearly understand the actions of these drugs.

Just cusping my mid-twenties, when my company was very young, I was coming back from a workout website video shoot with a client and I got a DUI in 2004, which I did not contest the charges. I learned I cannot legally drink *and* drive, especially over the limit. As a result, I must choose one or the other. My truck is Boss. Instead of drinking, I spend a day with Boss.

I find as I get older, my impulse towards intoxicants lessens. As a young man, I felt turmoil and torment and felt I never really got to be myself. As a result I was known at times of imbibement to go beyond healthy means. A girl who loved me during graduate school suggested a good guide would be to not be the only guy who showed up after drinking to an event where everyone else was sober. Her advice was loving and gentle and the first on the subject I thought to take.

I later briefly took up tobacco and the combination of lessening my exercise with drinking caused my waistline to swell. High blood sugar resulted and a concerted effort to taper my waist and avoid concentrated sugars has helped me to get my blood sugar back to healthy levels, now freer to remain there with only healthy diet and exercise, and lessened pharmaceutical drugs. It is a very nice feeling to go from the younger man, who may have done a little drinking even to the point of problems, to the more mature and wiser man who is pleased to show up. I feel as filmmakers, we can help who we are by presenting a healthier image system. I increasingly choose if I use intoxicants et al, and find I enjoy my sober moments with joy. I love to explore characters still struggling with such a decision, and allowing their system of society and support to be displayed. This support includes enabling.

SURRENDER

While I was in and out of heavy jungle, getting my Light Jungle Training in Panama,[7] I had befriended an indigenous species of Monkey known as a Riesling.[i] They are little gray monkeys who tend their own banana crops and eat bugs for protein. They also try to explain things in hands and faces, and do barter and trade. They taught me their flavor of storytelling. We understand what they are feeling and saying because we understand them as primates, and they will re-explain until we understand what they have tried to say. I found them generous and very soft to pet, with them admitting if they were clean enough for contact based on their own hygiene. Monkeys like to tell stories of exploits. They will indicate of their own adventures, and they will also tell the stories of others if they feel the story worth being shared.

One of the Rieslings, when we were found to be giving them veterinary, found me when some Naval Personnel were in the jungle, serving in the area near the Panama Canal.[8] The Monkey indicated his tooth was rotten.

---

[7] At the time defended by Army Rangers.

[8] The Navy was also conducting studies and we often saw them in the field. There is interest in an old Navy Hospital nearby.

Having had Wilderness survival training from the Boy
Scouts, I covered my mouth per training and looked at his
teeth. One was clearly rotten. I mentioned the tooth to the
navy, and, The Navy, in a study, extracted his tooth. Again,
the monkey had volunteered. He had entered into the
grove-area we were using in tremendous pain and when the
human dentist agreed with me, the tooth had to come out,
the dentist used an experimental tooth pull designed in case
an old-fashioned cannonball exploded and they had to pull
mass teeth, defined as over twenty. The navy had developed
the technology (which resembled an old-fashioned hand
drill) years ago, but never put it to use.

I explained to the Riesling, this is going to hurt and the
man from the Navy will pull his tooth out, and then he
won't be hurting anymore. The Riesling agreed to anything
so long as the effort stopped the pain. The dentist applied
the contraption and began turning the tool like an auger.
The Riesling, a wild animal but intelligent, tried to stay still.
He finally slumped his entire body and dropped his arms,
going totally limp. The strange process of having a human
care for him meant he wasn't in control, and he finally gave
in completely to being cared for. He had no other choice.

The tooth came out, and he half-scurried away and came
back to us in a near-panic, now realizing his tooth was gone.

10

He asked what to do, and we taught him to bite down on gauze. The Navy dentist had an issue on morality and ethics. Removing the tooth wasn't natural to the Riesling and any use of Antibiotics would have been experimental. I pointed out, with ethics, we wouldn't leave a human without antibiotic care. Plus, the guy is in the jungle. He had agreed the monkey needed care. We also needed to study new anti-biotics.

We put the issue to Army Ethics. We found, when we took the ethics bump, the pharmaceutical companies lined up to let the army even present the choice of experimental antibiotics to him, the Riesling physique being so much closer to ours than Guinea Pigs. The dentist picked an anti-biotic which was up for study and explained to the monkey what it did. He clarified with me, "He wouldn't get infected."[9] I agreed.

The Monkey accepted the prescription and took them every day with the same prescription strength as a human. He showed up voluntarily and admitted how glad he was to have had care. He had surrendered to us on the issue, due to pain. Surrender isn't giving up, surrender is giving in. Your characters may struggle with this.

---

[9] They do, undoubtedly, know what infection looks like.

SELF–ACTUALIZATION

Manifesting the Goals we set to is a form of Self–Actualization. Sharing Goals with others and seeing them through is a similar, but distinguishable thing. Having our unique efforts and goals benefit the entirety of the whole is another form of self–actualization. The Philosopher and Social Scientist Maslow has put his theories on this subject[10] into one of his two major premise goals, Hierarchy of Needs and his writings specifically on Self-Actualization. In his well–stated theories, Self–Actualization refers to what a person's full potential is and the realization of that potential.

These concepts, in my feelings, highly aid the understanding of social thoughts and societal goals and measures. Maslow brought forward empathetic feeling. These theories have grown more adeptly wielded and other have added to them with sophistication. Modern theories of enlightenment utilize them, and are to me, highly useful in

---

[10] They are summarized in the following heavily redacted example: Physiological needs, the physical requirements for human survival. Safety needs including: Personal security, Financial security, Health and well-being, Safety net against accidents/illness and their adverse impacts. Love and belonging such as: Friendship, Intimacy, Family. Esteem, or the typical human desire to be accepted and valued by others. Self-actualization referring to what a person's full potential is and the realization of that potential.

practice. I intend to include them in my cinema as innocuously as possible. Again, your characters may struggle with these goals.

Ken Wilbur advanced a theory of Social Spiral Dynamics[11], I believe to be self-actualizing. Wilbur felt we see children evolve from magical/mystical to logical and later humanist and inclusive. He thought all people as individuals go through these goals.[12]

Obviously, Ken Wilbur's theories are based on Chris Cowan and Don Beck, but Wilbur takes the measure into personal development, similar to how I have taken the theories of Joseph Cambell beyond academic introspection and analysis and into demonstrable professional and personal creativity. Wilbur has gone on to write with Beck when they took interest in each other's theories. Wilbur's efforts thus far have mostly focused on his readers gaining

---

[11] Spiral Dynamics suggests we as a society spiral in a system of peaks and plateaus into a more permanent enlightenment. The system originally put forward in a book called Spiral Dynamics by Don Beck and Chris Cowan described social evolution of society. The concepts were based on the theory of psychology professor Clare W. Graves. Ken Wilbur took the concepts of Cowen and Beck and then made them personal in evolution.

[12] As to the issue of inclusion of previous levels, one of my Professors at USC, Edo Stern, interestingly responded to the posing of the question of why so many video games show magic by suggesting we as humans "avoid the technology" by imagining magic.

enlightenment, and his own efforts. With Beck he extends beyond the self. I feel this is still an example of Self–Actualization, also.

FINDING INNER PEACE

Being content with both the internal and external chaos is necessary for a person to truly find peace. Neither denying what is nor embracing what isn't allows for a person to be reconciled, serene and still.

Feng Shui translates to Wind Water. The practice is to deftly choose surrounding oneself with a "feeling set" controling chaos and order in life[13]. Much of Asia embraces these theories. I find benefit to their practice.

Beyond our surroundings and into ourselves, I believe the Buddha, believed to be a teacher of peace, would love us to put the good thoughts in our head. I am trying to do the same in human endeavor, and with such, I am content with myself. Your characters may struggle with these issues.

---

[13] The feeling set has several different theories on pronouncing material in life to create effect based on goal. The effect can be profound when masterfully done, and palpable

FINDING CALM

I had an opportunity to spend some time in a Zen Garden at a monastery in Los Angeles. I found, as the city moved around me, so did a monk. He didn't know why I was there and became alarmed. The leading figure was their abbott-nun and she continued to find me pleasant despite the monk's increasing desperation. She knew me to be a friend of the Theravada and felt me welcome. He finally rejected her, instead reveling in the amount of commotion my calm presence had brought. I refused to fight him, not normally one to back down from a fight. They were all Japanese speaking, and my being there, invited or otherwise, was more than he could endure.

She later expressed fondness for me, and the Monk chose to move to another place. She admitted he had been hurting their Zen. She admitted I had sought calm[14]. The monk wasn't calm despite his training. According to the Nun, Calm is recognizing contentment is bare. I am quite fond of her also, and I still enjoy our friendship.

---

[14] Zen is oneness with what is.

FINDING JOY

A feeling resonates from the person which is exhilarating and euphoric. As the Dalai Lama states in The Art of Happiness, begin with contentment and then perhaps joy can arise. Joy can be palpable, and felt to originate from the heart-chakra.[15] With a practiced mind, joy shouldn't need to be short-lived. The more-practiced the mind, the easier the holding of arisement. A concept of the Four Immeasurables is to pray: May all sentient beings have happiness and its causes, May all sentient beings be free of suffering and its causes, May all sentient beings never be separated from bliss without suffering, May all sentient beings be in equanimity, free of bias, attachment and anger.

A basic of Buddhism is the clinging and attachment to the feeling of Joy can cause the ache of absence. This path was taught by the original Buddha, and is practicable. The accurate goal from the teachings I have received from the Theravada is to adhere is the dhamma (teachings of the Buddha). Again, the preferred advice is to be calm and still and breathing healthily and to recognize in the perfect moment, nothing is lacking. Finding Joy from this point is

---

[15] For the Christian set: Joy, Joy, Joy, Joy down in my heart.

much easier, even if the surrender needed to be here was difficult.

THE ZEITGEIST

We, as a culture, depend on shared images, words and experiences as the basis of communication, which at length is us sharing the experiences we have experienced and the thoughts we have contemplated as an individual to a larger socially aggregate totality. These are sometimes described as a wünderbërgerstüht, or a zeitgeist. Within ourselves as enjoyers of such community and belief, we are unique broadcasters of our beliefs and unique members of the shared sum total. I am aware Karl Marx asked questions in *Das Kapital*, and yes, I am aware this man's army has answers to all of his questions.

Zeitgeists change as time goes by[16]. Zeitgeists are perceptible, often charged with emotion. The Zeitgeist is rife with thoughts of belief and control. Even Architecture or literature forms, my own film movement included, seek to establish boundaries and goals. The Zeitgeist is a manipulative belief form. Zeitgeists are functional, even without our knowledge, of forming out actions and words. Zeitgeists are fundamental to the shape and structure of what we find acceptable. Often, people who share a Zeitgeist understand topics better than wording suggests. An example is Sharia law in the Muslim world in which classes and theories on the subject are taught, but mostly people know how they feel. For me, in the laws of Sharia, I'd hope to remember the rules. Both that which offends us and that which we aspire towards are based in the Zeitgeist.[ii] Language can bound Zeitgeist, as can tradition and religion.

As laws change, Zeitgeists change also. I think of the Williamses, Hank and Hank Jr. During the debates on desegregation, The Justice Department put an involatorum on use of common language such as the word "Negro."

---

[16] For example, my mentioned predecessor as Master Horseman of the Fifth Cavalry, Theobolt, had memories from the transition of the Army of the Great War to the Army of WWII and later Korea, Vietnam, and Desert Shield/Storm. Many changes took place in his time at my position. He was the first to believe he didn't need to defend segregation militarily.

They later stumbled with the word "Unsegregation" to overcome their own involatorum. The nation was in heated debates and Hank Williams gave his point of view. Williams spoke in a way he felt respectful when, on national television talking about the plight of the "Negro Worker," he used the banned term "Negro." I have seen the aired footage and I think he felt he was honestly trying to use the term in a sensitive way. Considering that TV station had "Blacks only and Whites Only" on their restrooms, was Hank Williams so rude to have brought up his sympathy to the plight of the blacks, with sensitivity?

A very well known quote from a Justice Department Official shows the government's transparent feelings on the subject. "We are not discussing desegregation. We are discussing segregation." The quotee went on to say that she felt that the use of the word "negro" was offensive to decency. The same Justice Department woman had a joke about the Klu Klux Klan. "They have a robe about her size." The national censors had placed an involatorum on the use of the word, and the authorities took the opportunity to punish Willams. Publicly, the Justice Department officially came down on the famous country music performer with the full force of the media control of the government. They

forced him to a national apology. They later acknowledged
the acknowledgement.

His son, Hank Williams Jr. later avoided compliance with
an involium with a drug reference in the sixties to marijuana
after a DEA moratorium on the use of the word.[17] Hank
Williams Jr. put forwards his feelings on them both being
singled-out in the raucous song, *Family Tradition*. My own
feelings in notice to the acknowledged-acknowledgement of
the Justice Department, with regard to segregation and
effect, we now enjoy a black president with the Audacity of
Hope.

A Zeitgeist is a bounding of cultural exchange. Zeitgeist
is sometimes defined as shared belief and sometimes thought
of as palpable belief. National zeitgeist is defined as the
hopes and dreams of the people. In a rebellious structure,
Zeitgeist is characterized as something we revolt and resist
against. Near-Professional propaganda suggests, join me in
the revolution. Professional propaganda instructs "We are
the Revolution." Your characters can struggle with these
goals.

---

[17] amongst other drug-names.

CROSSING BOUNDARY

Sometimes tools in propaganda allow for massive, global, zeitgeist change.[18] An example of massive zeitgeist shift is the Protestant reformation, in which the dominant Catholics were challenged in their efforts to ban books by radical thinkers such as the theologian and former monk Martin Luther, who eventually presented a bible in his common language of German. He is famous for his presentation of the trinity theory of "Father, Son and Holy Spirit," which outpaced the theory in Catholicism of "Mary, Mother of

---

[18] At all times of Government Acquiescence to revolution, examples England and Spain losing colonies, the rebellion against the standing government made the holding of those nations more expensive than their worth. No doubt, holding by force has been shown profitable in human history, but propaganda and violence often make the world change.

God." His theories put effort to include Native American religion which believed "The Great Spirit." Luther fought the establishment to gain the ability to present knowledge they found heretical and was eventually denounced by the Holy Roman Catholic Church. He challenged not only tradition, but also social moral practice.

Martin Luther's Protestant Theories reached across national and language boundaries, thereby affecting more than one Zeitgeist. He existed in the times of Gallileo Gallilei and Sir Isaac Newton. Gallileo challenged known proof of the world and Isaac Newton, Father of Modern Science, Concluded with Repeatable, Observable, Demonstratable theory. Luther considered them contemporaries in a different language, and therefore different sphere. He was an expert in crossing these spheres as is exemplified by the German Language Gutenberg Bible, declared both heretic and non-heretic as beyond the Latin of the Catholic Church[19]. The Heretic teachings took to massive uproar. Their traditions were challenged, and without tradition there was less to 'not-regard' and more to argue.[20]

---

[19] and less close to original writings in the Greek and the other language writings of the original disciples.

[20] Also, lay beneficiaries could argue scripture in their own language.

A Zeitgeist is more of an ethereal thing. Ethereal is understood as something which can be felt, shared and explained which is other than tangible, although sometimes manifest as ideas in physical, as in architecture styles which permeate building designs across an era. The thesaurus definition for ethereal is otherworldly. This may be extreme for the Zeitgeist.

For the Zeitgeist, ethereal suggests beyond tangible control. Modern theorists, however, do not believe such, even of personal belief. They believe thought can be formed. Even the state of deep suggestion can be trained. The key to deep suggestion is, often by force of will, write the ideas physically, overcoming the short term/long term memory process which separates dreaming from normal deep recall.[21] The writer must will himself or herself beyond comfort.[22]

While awake, many writers spend time in the depths of their remembrances and feelings. They may remember things they have said before, at this time of writing without

---

[21] The natural order of the written word overcomes the clutter of the suggestive state.

[22] Often writers deal with issues of shifting the zeitgeist, and deep suggestive state is able to be more connected to the zeitgeist whole than the normal conscious mind, as the zeitgeist whole is deeper than normal society. Obviously, a primal connection free of fear and judgement such as deep suggestion is an advantage to the writer.

others around who may have worded the initial wordings with them.[23] They are often deep in the Zeitgeist, which is reflective with thoughts and feeling patterns they have experienced before. In these dialogue remembrances, the writers have often added their beliefs to the exchanges they are detecting in the belief patterns, and relive them as they are creative towards a goal.

Pushing against the Zeitgeist often results in what the Buddhists have called Karmic Return. They refer to this return, thus I have heard, as The Law of Resultive Action. The basic of the concept as explained to me is that at least something changes with these efforts. At best, your beliefs take effect.

Almalgamatively, these changes and efforts can have a massive cumulative effect. You may believe this, I do believe this and I have given you something real. You can have effect on the world. Written words can change things. You can resist that which you are averse to and support wholeheartedly with effort that which you adore even to the point of violence and violent meditations.

Tradition is how we do things. Religion has observances and practice. Religion, in social control, is a tool. Writers

---

[23] I often went over my class notes this way when I was inappropriately kept away from them.

who are antisocial may endeavor to change the status quo to their own goals, often laboriously, fittingly described as chiseling the Zeitgeist. We have as a culture, come to believe, the pen is mighty and the sword is bent with age.

The effort of writers affects the Zeitgeist as a whole. If they, as a believer, are socially directed, they may choose to shift the Zeitgeist or add something new and well endorsed. They give themselves to the larger whole. Through actions of belief with intention, groups can change their Zeitgeist.[24]

Art shapes the Zeitgeist, especially as propaganda. Propaganda, as defined by me, is anything contemplatable with government approval, especially if disseminatable. Morality drives the propaganda machine and the propaganda machine decides what gets seen. Propaganda is either state sponsored, state supported, or state suppressed.

Beliefs and their place in writings in the Zeitgeist are what form the literary Zeitgeist. At least for the writers, the active use of the Zeitgeist is remembering and rekindling their strong beliefs. Often, strong beliefs, especially in youth, are instrumental in making an exceptional child believe that he or she can be a writer. Zeitgeist is at best

---

[24] This rarely changes the Zeitgeist in its entirety, which dates back to the earliest days of shared language. Individuals normally only add to the existing Zeitgeist with new theories or thoughts, which may become more well-acclimated by the people.

shared on the levels of agreement and feeling, and art fits
within these goals.

UPHEAVAL

The society often reflects on writers as to whether or not their work is one they can be proud of, as some writers have fantasy of fetish beyond the norm. One of the magicks of cinema is we can present a world where people would have been violent. Without knowledge of proper morals driving moral shifts, young writers try to sell the wrong goals. They may, in cinema as an example, pander to violence. They may not know that in official release, all killings showed in films need to go through a clearing to comply with actual global lethal legal, otherwise, the depictions of the kills aren't allowed. We want to encourage society.

Killing is taking someone's life, so they aren't alive anymore. In the real world this leaves bereaved and a corpse and the legal of a death certificate. This is a major event. In official propaganda, these subjects are not taken lightly. This concept resonates to innate morality, similar to how we wouldn't show a boxer cheating in a film on boxing and hold him up as a hero[25]. In our genuine feeling, we naturally agree heroes are to be upheld. Violence has result. Good guys out maneuver bad guys; the establishment shifts for good.

We as media makers have a responsibility in portrayal. We should honestly depict the issues of killing. For example, if a marine claims he has killed six people, he needs to have killed six people of he is a liar. Bottom line, did he initiate ending six peoples' lives? Show the truth in the movie.

Connected people from salesmen to politicians use predictable demographics to quietly control messages to the masses. Thus I have heard from the Buddhists, life is characterized by suffering: Birth is characterized by suffering, Adolescence is characterized by suffering, Old Age is characterized by suffering, Death is characterized by suffering. The government takes these predictable opportunities we all endure in our own lives and the lives of

---

[25] unless he is fighting another cheating boxer

those near us to instill national and social bents and goals.[26]
The society at these ages is open and willing to both discuss
the media and adapt the mores. Governments use this
willingness to selfish benefit of self-perpetuation and also
social benefit of social settlement such as reduce crime,
reduce upheaval, reduce reluctance and reduce apathy.
When contemplating leadership and right, honesty always
factors.[iii]

The Zeitgeist troubles some people. They endeavor to
shift the zeitgeist beyond official national control. Often
feeling they are forward thinkers, they seek to not be stuck
in a pattern they cannot govern. They often become
motivated thinkers, trying their best to force their way into
another mode of thought. They often endeavor to manifest
their will with their beliefs. Sometimes this yields result in
thought provocation such as Aristotle, Socrates and Plato.
These men practiced ideas into radical shift and Aristotle
who taught Alexander the Great went on to changing the
known world with the reign of Alexander. As open
propagandasmith with clear training, I have knowledge of
Alexander the Great and Plato, who put forward the first
formal propaganda written for dispersal, intentional and

---

[26] This alone doesn't mean they are corrupt, although maybe overly secretive.

military in goal. They offered, in all known languages, the announcement "Alexander has taken Athens." Alexander the Great even offered education systems in all conquered languages where his subjects learned to read their language in the process, where his magnificent successes were taught formally, including him and his army taking their city. Many indigenous of those regions still thank him for teaching words.

Another example closer to our time, Civil Disobedience by Henry David Thoreau put forward a structure of lawful defiance, lesser than rebellion but higher in form. This book endeavors to put forward a track to guide creative efforts within the zeitgeist, more functional than insurgency and more honest in goal. Civil Disobedience still enjoys massive readership in what began as an explanation of why Thoreau rejected pole-taxes.

Propaganada is generally designed with one of two goals in mind: One is to stifle effort or change and the other is to inspire effort or change. Professional propaganda, well designed, is generally able to do both at the same time, although normally obviously pointed with "main force" in one direction or the other. Propaganda that encourages is normally called positive propaganda. Propaganda that discourages is normally called negative propaganda. Positive propaganda can instill long–standing changes and betterment of efficiency in shared goals. Our society needs these upheavals. Hopefully, increasingly, increasingly good cultures are what we do openly.

INTELLIGENT DESIGN

Propaganda and intent are often defended by the military. Well-made propaganda moves-and-affects Zeitgeist on-purpose. Governments approve propaganda for this goal of Zeitgeist enforcement and social structure. For example, the Motion Picture Association of America allows motion picture ratings to encourage age specific concepts and images. Through ratings[27], the government is able to finesse message and tool 'image detail' to a demographic that has predictable troubles and turmoil. Zeitgeist, Trouble, and

---

[27] The M.P.A.A. is a voluntary structure, but, since theater owners and traditional rental venues comply to the rating system, the voluntary structure is strong enough to control the masses. I, as a professional filmmaker, voluntarily comply to the now somewhat archaic Hayes Production Code understanding that for a fee, the MPAA will list the level of restriction. On this level, the Hayes code is still very real and modern filmmakers are liberated by the openly restrictive ratings. I combine their old rules with the safety of the MPAA system, which allows me the structure of their guidelines opening the screen again to images which are sexual, or violent, or disruptive.

Turmoil entwine at the level of dilemma, and demographics often have predictable dilemmas that share spending and seeking-of-answer patterns. First kisses and first loves only happen once in a person's life.

We have a certain expectation of a film if we see the rating attached. Restricted means, according to the old rules, the film is limited to the age of majority. PG means, parental guidance may be needed as a child may have questions as to the subject matter, for example death of a loved one or the stability of a family being upset by a parent having a job loss. PG-13 ratings often result when a writer isn't concerned with ratings and the studio tem them back to appeal to a broader demographic with disposable income. G means General Audience, and considering how modern children may watch the same film over and over again, and parents watch and enjoy these films also, writers may actually have the largest affect by appealing to the largest and most impressionable level of the Zeitgeist: Children and their learning environment.

The Zeitgeist can be a tool for a writer as, if the writer is learned, with the Zeitgeist the writer has ideas to draw upon and a place for their idea's worth to be reflected. Writers and believers put real effort into these reflections. Writers of imaginative and new concepts can often affect the Zeitgeist.

Before they are written, if the writing is significant, the Zeitgeist aches for the writing. After they are written, the writings can fill a palpable hole. I find this similar to a physics theory by J.S. Bell called non-locality in which Bell proved mathematically objects do not need to be near each other in time or space to affect each other. Similarly, in a modern Zeitgeist, ideas do not need to be near each other in language or region in order to affect each other and our special super-global whole. For example, we still emanate to antiquity and before, and their contributions still resonate with us. We can rent movies from Japan and distribute in China.

If a screenwriter's work resonates to a morality you feel at your core, their work will be ready for what we in the Hollywood structure call, "slate shifts." Slate shifts are when the studios change the production order which is normally set up, at least in general broad strokes, a decade or so in advance. Surprises, such as the attacks on September 11th, 2001 often make the studios change the projects they have had planned to release. Having been a script reader at the time for an Academy Award winning producer, I know so many of the planned movies were like *The Matrix* or *Fight Club*, some Guy comes in and does damage to the place. This wasn't as cool immediately after 9/11.

Often, a new morality is sought and new projects, even if old scripts, get considered. They are sometimes frantic if they are ashamed of the scripts they had put forward.

If slate shifts happen without predictability, and slate shifts are when projects are purchased and moved forward, writers are smartest and most true to themselves to not only put forward morality, but to put forward their own morality. Even if people tell you the concepts will never sell, as a writer you are best served to provide the types of Thoughts, Ideas, and Beliefs you would like to see and have an audience experience.

Currently, and while on topic of the old goal, hearts and minds, my efforts are mostly media. I have sincere issues with portrayal. I know Propaganda reflects a culture and the disparateness between America and the other nations of the world grows more extreme. We weren't, coming from an American export point-of-view, getting media release in Muslim Nations and eventually the extreme of disparity grew to extremism. They found us immoral. Europe, as an opposent example, found us too tame, and also reliant on profound violence.

All people benefit in living life with moral fortitude. As Ghandi stated, "Be the change you want to see in the world." Writers will feel better about the work they present and their work, at least to themselves, will defy criticism. They will also be more ready if there is any upset or social upheaval.

The old patriotic values and virtues machine nurtures solidarity and growth. We promote adherence and unity in effort. This mechanism is often utilized to guide and aim society. This direction makes us who we are, on level, caring about virtue, vice, anger, sugar and spice, and everything regarding social ascension. In America, we value democracy, responsibility, response ability, and adjustable mores. We aggressively consume media and propaganda and have an insatiable appetite for what is new. We feed the appetite.

Using my own words, if we speak to something primal within our self, we extend beyond the conscious mind and into a thought collective we can understand to be larger than any one person, thought process, religion, or selfish goal. We enter our talent, power, genius and offerings into the collective Zeitgeist.

STORY AND TOOLS

One of the most sincere ways we discern how early man distinguished himself from the animals is through his use of tools. Tools, to an anthropologist, are often defined by their function.

Story is a type of tool. At society's dawn, the tool "Language" quickly began to permeate our culture and our thoughts, and as language permeated our thoughts, so did language permeate our ideas. We eventually acknowledged language to take on structure and form and we began to teach ourselves things both in history and mores. As mankind increasingly became able to express increasingly complex thoughts, our methods for maintaining them increased in sophistication. Examples are drama, written calligraphy, cryptographic language and rhyming poem, as well as even more advanced form such as lyrics and songs. As language and storytelling evolved, language tools and remnants of stories became some of our most prized examples of how we as a modern society came to be.

To our best standards, the sophistication of a society is often viewed on the level of the intertwining of art and tools, especially when we also consider the artistry of weapons and killing. We judge a society by art and science and the art of culture dissemination. Propaganda presentation is a tool of elegance, increasingly evident at goal setting.

I recognize propaganda as real, and I define anything in contemplatable media with government approval to be propaganda, especially if disseminatable. I feel Propaganda and the proliferation of propaganda can be considered art and tool, and this book deals with their entanglement.

As artists, we choose what we offer. As consumers we choose what we receive. We may teach and gift our children and ourselves with ever more sufficing morality, concepts and thoughts that shape who we choose to become. Propaganda and social goal are system and tool. I honestly feel, propaganda is at it's best heartfelt, yet I also believe fundamental morality is a concept in writing. As a society, quality in media benefits from meritorious artistic endeavor and socially altruistic goals from the heart of the artist.

Obviously, quality is a goal most writers strive towards. Julia Cameron, in her book "The Artist's Way" suggests successful artists let God worry about the Quality, and the artist should worry about the Quantity. This is well stated and does get the words moving without criticism, one of the goals of The Artist's Way.

Know for an artist, more than one goal may be useful in getting both quality and quantity into the project as deftly as intended. Understanding and expressing the story is more important at writing than knowing when the audience may like the work. You never know who will find your work enjoyable. If you are motivated to create, why even bother to second guess yourself? If you feel inspired, create. You will never get as much done if you belabor writing instead of at least jotting furiously in the moment of inspiration.

FREE MOVIES

I believe, and the Army agrees with me, I am allowed to
be a soldier and also endeavor. My main endeavor[28] is the
Cinema-Libre, based in Direct Cinema and Cinéma-Vérité.
You notice all of the movements of the like mentioned in
the book, even in name, all emphasize not accepting
obstacles. The intent of Cinéma-Vérité was to show truth[29]
and the goal of Direct Cinema was to Direct Cinema.
Sometimes, a society advances beyond expectation as is seen
in the sixties when television had more people wanting to
stay home for entertainment. Even traditionally successful

---

[28] and the operation of my production company Vision Quest Entertainment Incorporated

[29] Which Jean Rouch found personal, meaning "me" for him. For all, the Egoic sentience is desperate
to thrive and use every tool available.

genres of cinema began to flounder. The studios looked to younger and younger directors to reach an audience that was increasingly disenfranchised with the traditional cinema fare. More information is available on this in the film "Easy Riders, Raging Bulls"[30]

Film movements have existed before which do not have rules attached to them, and are nearly as old as cinema itself. The Early Russian Experiments grew to increasingly sophisticated methods of portrayal which trancended national boundaries and are the building blocks of the modern cinema. The Hollywood Model is not immune as we see in the original founding of United Artists and the eventual rebellion by talent against management and their controls.

For me, as an artist, I have adopted artistic tenets as one my tools. My tenets are known as the Cinema-Libre Tenets. They borrow most heavily from the interpreted statements of Cinéma-Vérité[31], the French Film Movement which followed World War II, founded by filmmaker Jean

---

[30] Book Also.

[31] The Third Tenet of the Cinema-Libre states: All Cinema-Libre Filmmakers should, whenever possible, use the tenets expressed by Cinéma-Vérité Filmmakers, combining both ideals to create the Cinema of Truth and Freedom.

Rouch, and with the third of my three tenets I acknowledge this borrowing. The First Tenet denies the existence of something very real: Money. The goal of the denial is to allow art to flourish without the feeling of being downtrodden. In ancient days, people migratory or otherwise, stuck to their water supplies and their goals to be happy. Nowadays we have convinced people they need money to be happy. If making a film makes you happy, make a film your goal.

Money is defined by me as something perceived of value, used in barter[32]. At a point of distribution with a finished film, boxed and saleable, edited and met, I know I no longer feel like the film is still being made. I don't mind money there. Once the film is made, at the point of distribution, I no longer feel I am the filmmaker. I am now a property holder to whatever extent I have held point[33], and there isn't doubt money exists at this stage, until we as a species have instituted something radically different in the future. As to the tenets, the rules are barely flexible but applicable.

---

[32] Remember, I am a military anthropologist, and we consider what has been shown effective, even to ancient tactics.

[33] More information is available in the legal section of A Writer's Guide to the Hero's Journey: A Handbook for Screenwriting in the Cinema-Libre Film Movement

Film budgets begin as imaginary estimates. Sometimes a million, here or there, wows audiences enough to earn extra millions at the box office. Resources, well placed, can make a huge difference, and are sometimes difficult to estimate. I re-iterate, the budgets are imaginary at first, later (at the end of the day/week/month accrue) the money is real, but then spent. To the filmmaker at the budget stage, (i.e. line producer), money does not exist, but is still a reality. In the "expert set," if you need the pan-lock set-well[34], spare no expense. Again, to the filmmaker, money does not exist[35].

Several of the more well-established names I know well (mostly actresses) may kindly acquiesce to my complex model of money's existence on set, but to agents, managers and eventually talent, everyone expects to get paid.

Everyone fights for points and credit, actors, producers, writers, etc. and while he still needn't feel downtrodden, I admit a satisfaction if a screenwriter i.e. comes to me wanting to get paid, and he has to settle to goal[36] enough to

---

[34] or any other gizmo

[35] To gain believability, I iterate, we would like to make money after the film is made. We have a model for profit where, even before theatre cost and release, we make $500,000 if we invest six million through an exclusive sales arrangement with DishNetwork they have acknowledged.

[36] Similar to a soccer player who gets an assist at a goal-opportunity.

admit he isn't the filmmaker. A Filmmaker puts the film on the wall. I do however, agree with the Writer's Guild, writers wrote that movie, but I feel when the concept is a "Go-Picture" I don't want any more finagling about money. Let's get the film up and on the wall.

Hollywood is a bloodthirsty game. For every 1,000 ideas, roughly 100 get written, 10 get bought and one gets made. The same skills taught me by the army provide ability in Hollywood. Also, the Army is pleased I increased effluence in large budgets by even contemplating the millions of dollars alloted to most films, without infringing on their own similarly sized budgets.[37] I wasn't re-inventing their wheel to learn how to spend this much money.

In military Anthropology "Why is he doing that?" isn't the same as the more academic "How he is doing that." We would most likely at least agree actions are intentional and should have possible benefit of activity towards goal.[iv] This book and the Tenets are both meant to instruct as to the "Why" of the "Why is he doing that?" and also to the how, when the model begins to show success.

---

[37] Police, National Guard General, Marines, Seals, Etc. have all transpired on this effluence.

THE TENETRY

The Tenets of the Cinema-Libre are meant for both the general audience and the filmmakers to be an additional point of debate and thought-founding, as well as found to be an encouraging point of comparison for other humanities.

1) To the Cinema-Libre Filmmaker, money does not exist. Cinema-Libre is an expression of pure creativity, free of fears of profitability and commerciality. All filmmakers and films working under the Cinema- Libre Code should recognize the divine state of being and that state's innate ability to create everything from nothing. In this creator's image, all skills, materials, talent, lighting elements, design elements, production equipment and other tools must be native to the artists, borrowed from friends or liberated. Manual labor

and other working as a bartering tool is strongly encouraged as the Cinema–Libre Filmmaker is expected to be of service.

2) All films created under the Cinema–Libre Code must be as positive as possible in nature, with the heroes representing loving–kindness and the beauty, truth, and difficulty natural to the state of the human condition. They should further teach tested and real techniques to the audience for the liberation from worldly suffering, as best understood by the filmmakers, including: meditation, presence, communion, forgiveness, sobriety, surrender, self–actualization and finding inner peace, calm, and joy.

3) All Cinema–Libre Filmmakers should, whenever possible, use the tenets expressed by Cinéma–Vérité Filmmakers, combining both ideals to create the Cinema of Truth and Freedom.

The First Tenet of the Cinema–Libre puts forward a goal of collaboration, with each of the listed elements and aims suggested to have at least one person in charge of them. The tenet gives an approach to manifesting the cinema where there is no one to blame and no reason to be rejected.

The Second Tenet of the Cinema–Libre allows for discourse of what is good in storytelling, including the type of storytelling we uphold as a species, even to our children.

The Second tenet allows for a peaceful contemplation of aim, and media projects which make the American Spectacle of Cinema more palatable to international audiences which require moral interplay with open debatability, and often a media level acceptable to the audiences expectations of raucousness and dilemma.

The Third Tenet of the Cinema-Libre opens the filmmakers to reality and liberation. Jean Rouch sought to improve France. We put similar measure to the world. We also note in modern cinema, the Digital Versatile Disc, Blu-Ray or otherwise, allows us to have more honesty with our audience by showing them the magic tricks in cinema, special effects and etc. et al., in the bonus features. Also, Using *Schindler's List* and *Saving Private Ryan* as brilliant examples, on the Third Tenet first off:

1. Do they have a location?
2. Are they a period piece (Equipment, uniforms, tactics, etc.)?
3. Was their effort to try to portray these things accurately?

Speaking as a propagandasmith, what I am most impressed by with the Filmmakers in the Cinéma-Vérité is their ardor to take Post-Global War Chaos and defiance and turn their feelings into their still watchable efforts of film.

Cinéma-Vérité led to the narrative films of the French New Wave.[38] For the French filmmakers of the era, their psyches are the products of war. In their post-war feelings they are French, and they as French Men stood against aggression and survived to making their movies. They are based in Direct Cinema, which is based in Kino-Pravda. The French and Global culture and their fortitude after the war allowed these men to present cinema they felt to be true. For the Cinéma-Vérité and the filmmaking of the French New Wave, they put something forward they as Frenchmen resonated to and felt.

Cinéma-Vérité states: "Il y a deux façons de concevoir le cinéma du réel : la première est de prétendre donner à voir le réel; la seconde est de se poser le problème du réel. De même, il y avait deux façons de concevoir le cinéma vérité. La première était de prétendre apporter la vérité. La seconde était de se poser le problème de la vérité."

Assisted Translation: "There are two ways of conceiving the real cinema: the first is to pretend to give-and-take to see the real and the second is to stage the problem of the reality. Similarly, there were two ways of understanding cinema

---

[38] In part due to the legal precedent of Jean Rouch and his contract with the French Government.

49

truth. The first was to pretend to purport the claim to truth. The second was to pose the problem of truth.

A good friend of mine, Devon Winter, whom I founded my first Production Company, Left of Center with, once teased me of my intelligence and goals. "Does anyone know anything about the French New Wave?" He joked, pretending to be on a movie set as though the impasse was holding back their progress. Devin was one of the few friends I had with more set experience than me at the time. He started as a grip, known for his hustle and clean return to start.[39]

Teasing endured, I do use my tenets as tools, and I lean on them whenever I, as a writer, am seeking the next thing in my storytelling to do or show. Cinema-Libre begins with an acceptance of Cinéma-Vérité. The rules of the Cinema-Libre are meant to be embodied, especially at writing[40] and editing.

Even with the above believed true, Art for the sake of art isn't enough for me. I encourage goals and even beyond desire, I insist upon viewership and vulnerability. Simply stated, viewership means people both watch and enjoy my

---

[39] Grips return to a safe-position between takes to be ready and to not interfere with the shot.

[40] Which influences production.

films. I would allow you as a viewer, and should you be a filmmaker, a similar enjoy-ability.

HOLLYWOOD

In Hollywood, the tradition is to describe even female protagonists as the hero. The old logic was they didn't want to keep writing "Hero or Heroine" but the reality also is most films made in the past have had males as leads. In our efforts to bring about a new cinema, there is no reason for us to not give women characters their due. I quote Olivia Wilde, as to what she said in the book by Ramin Setoodeh about my friend Paul Haggis[41] and women in Hollywood:

"This is what studios need to realize, and are realizing, with the success of 'Hunger Games,' 'Twilight' and 'The Fault is in our Stars,': It's so clear that audiences will flock to

---

[41] Screenwriter of *Crash* and *Million Dollar Baby*.

see female-driven films. It's not a niche market. We aren't a minority."

We may recognize the tradition but also strive for the new. This is an example of character as tool. When you flesh and fill your writing with archetypes or characters, which are purely entertaining and fun, they make your film, play, or poem more enjoyable and universal, entertaining a larger audience where entertainment is the goal. Most great films mix in an ample amount of substance.

On issues of representation, Hollywood, if they even address the issue, has traditionally gone overboard to the point of tip-toeing near offensiveness. I would like to see a world where people of morality can be sensitive and genuine; a cinema where we present characters of interest, and also learning and example. We have a very important role socially in cinema, and I believe in Nirvana, all people could share stories regardless of cultural or language barriers. My rules constitute rules.

There is a fine line between archetype and stereotype. I'd like us to respect this as we try to write characters of other races, genders, faces, creeds and codes.[42] If we don't know

---

[42] A Buddhist at the bowl might set his food down right when he has the urge, "I'd like to eat more of this." At that point he still has more. If we measure our rice by eye, we have much to swallow.

them, how can we write them well? How do we reveal them realistically and accurately? Believably?

Films at least have the shine from their talent on the sophisticated people and images we are allowed to know, even sometime feeling intimate when their face is forty feet tall on the screen. Talent can never be underestimated. Actors and actresses are even more valuable than their box office draw because they are a path, when attached, to finance and culmination.

Hollywood is an adjusters game. Each film needs to breath and be given life. Each film needs attention. Each film needs roots and wings. One to hold the film to the earth, and the other to let the shimmering light and sound go free.

I love having support from the women in this industry. More than a handful of times, I have been near a film with strong males attached, and I close to production with a starlet. I love my girls and one of the SAG actresses all the way back to my film school thesis admitted why I am considered so different. "You are honest with me and we both want me to look great. I trust you with me."

PRODUCTION

In economics and also formal economics, words can be functionally maturated. The following principles exist in economics, in which I am trained: Driving willpower, demand, demand structure, commodity goal, and fathom. Fathom is ideas driven to goal. Fathom is commodifiable and if a thing in economics is commodifiable, the thing is mathematically studiable and demonstratable. In Economics, the less something costs, the more we didn't have to spend. This goes for labor and materials as well as planning, operation and goal. The obvious opposite is the more something costs, the more we would be forced to implement–spend to expropriate, expritiate or expreciate.

The more specific the goal, the more functional the endeavor. Likewise, the best path of endeavor always means

putting the most effort towards the goal.[43] No project
which requires long term commitment and possibly
additional manpower can be completed without the goals at
least being defined, and at best shared and understood.
These defined goals are particularly useful when involved in
the processes of collaboration and shared effort. Film, for
example, is a collaborative artform. Many people need to
work together and contribute their unique expertise. By the
time all of the elements are in place, every location is
permitted and everything pictured has given release for their
image and all of the subjects have given release for their
story. All of the costumes and vehicles are given placement,
and any architecture especially if there is destruction, has
been cleared. Even ambiences and sounds need to be cleared
and eventually, music and any pictured images. Nothing
happens accidentally.

In regards to this intentionalism, John Williams has a
fairly famous quote as to the jarringness of sound and score in
cinema. "In both Indiana Jones and the Trelismo in Star
Wars, sound arouses existence and subtly backs down to the
action. In Star Wars, at the awards ceremony, Sound is
announced as existing diagetically (in the world of the

---

[43] And solution.

characters). The sound stays prominent and reminds us
lovingly, we are in the world of Star Wars." Notice in this
example, everything is intentional and designed.

The production of a film generally uses the script as a
blueprint for the project and professional production will
almost always allow the script's being acted-and-filmed to
function as the initial production goal. In other words,
putting the script on film is why they showed up that day.
By this standard, at the writing stage the screenplay is both a
goal and a tangible thing, which will eventually be used as a
goal standard at the next level of execution. Can you
fathom?

At the pay-or-play level, the studio has invested money
into the above the line artists and will advance the project to
the production stage to offset their liability as pay-or-play
means the artists will get paid whether or not the project gets
up. Money at this level is already essentially lost, so the only
way to make any profit is to take the film all the way to
release. This obviously also involves successful edit.

There are people who invest and people who put the
movie on the wall. You don't need money to create. That
said, production is even more work than writing. As more
capital is risked to move through production, the only
reason to really make the film is because you really want to,

and, although difficult to guess, potentially see a market on the other side.[44] To be truly free of a money concept limiting, a young filmmaker may be better served to start with a short story first. Know these rarely make money, though, but at least they risk less. You, as you advance in your career, would at least have something to show. Even then, by the time a crew starts filming, they should be confident with the script.

---

[44] See my own shorts, *The Railord* and *Burned All the Way to the Edge.*

ONLY THE TALENTED

When an expert is able to create something new, many times the world isn't quite ready to receive from them. They are often asked to set their work aside for sometimes many years, where their own thoughts turn around and, of course, return. Often, the work is a greater collaboration between them and the world. I heard from an academy award-winning producer on the subject, when he was talking about how much effort is put into a work, which is ready for a billion people to see:

"The first effort is an abortion. The second one is an incubation. The third is the right to ready and the real is the ready is go." Al Ruddy stated the statement to me around 2001, referring to how many drafts of a work he expects to go through in order to see the effort up to his level of professional.

Some of the best advice I ever received on the subject of filmmaking came from Academy Award winner Albert S. Ruddy, whom I worked with in 2001 and 2002, who suggested to me as a young professional to have multiple products going at one time, all of them ready to go (meaning ready to be produced). He had suggested even concepts are useful, so long as you own them, and he had seen a lot of films go up by the time he shared his logic with me. Al had worked at Paramount pictures for several years and is now a two time Oscar winning producer. I was his story editor at the time he was approving the script for *Million Dollar Baby*. When I first started at his company after I had interned with Academy Award Winning Producer Gray Fredericksen, if either of them had written a publication, I would have read the book. Al stated, "One of the most misunderstood things in 'crass' Hollywood is the value of art. Al always wanted a script that was a perfect ten. What Gray wanted was a go picture.

When Al sold up *Million Dollar Baby*, he had two requirements for around the office to minimize fights in regards to how he and others feel. He righteously maintained he was "the Producer."[45] He also asserted and succeeded; he is credited in the film as such.

I was instrumental in many of Al's early decisions on *Million Dollar Baby* and he kindly acknowledged. For example, I was first to second his goals of keeping the characters he wanted, including the character later played by Morgan Freeman who is in a different part of the short story set by F.X. Toole of what was then called "Rope Burns" and is now called "Million Dollar Baby."

Al wanted Hillary Swank for the part she eventually won an academy award for. He didn't know how to get a hold of her. I knew Lisa Gottlieb, who was one of my film professors at the time, and the director of *Boys Don't Cry*. I talked to Lisa about the opportunity for Hillary and Lisa said, "I think Hillary would love the opportunity." She contacted Hillary and I got to send her the script, something I had the pleasure to do on a lot of projects with young talent interested and me covering hundreds of scripts Al would buy and then sell with talent or changes, or simply more momentum. Al wanted *Million Dollar Baby* all the way, and I got to be there when he attached Clint Eastwood and Morgan Freeman. He credited me with finding Hillary

---

[45] His assistant had a problem with this one, considering her own ambition.

Swank, who said, "I am very excited about this picture."
He was pleased, but at that level of bravisimo he said,
"Credit is earned in this business." I am in the Hollywood
Creative Directory as Story Editor for the Ruddy Morgan
Organization at the time, but I don't show in the picture
credits for *Million Dollar Baby.* I was bundled to the
acknowledgements.

I left the nest early, when $100,000 came up for my own
film, still in progress.[46] I wouldn't be surprised if Al shows
up on that one, too, one hundred years old or otherwise.
He had promised he would. "Keeping promises is part of
the biz." He stated. I believe him. He was sure I could have
stuck around for more credit and closer to the big time
show.

Al was famous when people in a meeting wanted their
way and stated their goal, and then, millions of dollars on the
line, listened and sought ammunition intellectually for their
cause. He would ponder, pose with poise, maybe tell a joke,
and show he wasn't in a hurry. They became exhausted.
He was having a meeting, they were all at their goals.

He said, "So many people short–lived in the biz take their
moment to make their 'their,' there." He added, "They

---

[46] A road movie I would love to have star Taylor Swift.

often leave their 'their,' there as well. "'Knowing the business is knowing the business. Knowing who is in the business is less important. People come back and go everyday. Every movie makes a different star. Who amongst them will be sought if there is a new project on the line? Only the talented." I loved hearing his stories, as he was always in the know.

Al and the master contractor, Frank Barnes, I had apprenticed under spoke briefly when I was working at Ruddy Morgan. Both men were geniuses of learning. With as much as he knew, Al also rarely hesitated to pick up something new. Even around the Beverly Hills office, I still talked about Frank, due in large part to his ample gifting. Al had taken interest in my upbringing. Frank taught me to know a tool. Al liked knowing and using tools, including the wield-of-knowledge.

A specific example came up when Al was working a side-opportunity with a smaller, slicker company he and Andre had formed called A&A productions. We were debating the size of a crane to rent. The cost wasn't the prohibitive, the aeracy of the land we were shooting on was and we needed to decide early if we were to accommodate both director and permit. Al wanted to give the director what he wanted. I offered up know-how.

As a young man, learning the craft of painter's apprentice and master contractor, I learned the value of clean tools. I learned the value of predictable tools, and I learned the value of diverse tools.[47] I also learned the value of a single go-to tool that is allowed to be a little dirty with the same color paint we are using for the length of the job. For a painter's apprentice, this is the 5-in-1 which is used for any scraping, cleaning, buffeting, gouging or prepping in which you want either or both the tool handy, or a tool you will not need to spend any extra time cleaning back to ready later. If the director is really going to use the fifty-foot crane, let the crane be his 5-in-1. Both of these lessons, diverse and go-to are valuable to me today and instrumental to the lessons taught in this book. Al found this type of logic so simple and therefore, very valuable. He wanted more for himself.

Al, who loved knowing men of knowledge, admitted he had become curious-enough and with my permission, called Frank. Al considered my younger knowledge of contracting very pertinent to film. Frank was pleased to hear from both

---

[47] One of the advantages of working with, for example, a Dremel tool: When deciding to rent a tool oe not, you can think, "What Dremel attachment would I use? Why don't I?" Should I rent a larger tool? If so, which one? Peruse the tools and attachments realizing you haven't spent any more money than you had yesterday. If you bought and contemplate them, they are probably close to the goal you have.

of us, and pleased I had found what he considered to be good employment.

When they spoke, Frank, a man who rarely shied on a "joke on-the-sly" raised the issue, is Albert S. Ruddy a Master Producer who could therefore take an apprentice? Al liked the title and said, "Yes." Frank allowed the newly christened master producer a few questions, some which Al had had since his teenage years.

Al asked, "When is a master cut different then a pro?"

"Never." Frank responded, totally confident. (Frank always got paid, even at Master.)

"When is a pro-cut worth the money?"

"Always." Otherwise the guy charged the wrong amount of money.[48]

Frank won the phone call. The phone call ended with Al sad. Frank had taught him so much, he could now answer a question he had had for years. The call ended up $76 of Domestic Long Distance (we were looking for a new plan). Al admitted Frank and the Marines (and Army). Al believes, if the military taught him to learn, he would have.

---

[48] I have learned a contractor may contemplate, "How deep, how cheap, how fast, how well done?"

GOALS

The Army taught me to build massive machines. I consider my film movement similar. The following types of measures can be applied to manpower actualization goals of the Cinema-Libre or any other endeavor:

Cost: What is the commitment financially to the goal? A Famous saying in Hollywood is "Nothing is as cheap as paper." The quote suggests things can always be done less expensively at the planning stage. Would manpower need money or would they work without pay like many amateurs in Hollywood who will work for "Copy, Credit and Meals?"[49] Are costs you have estimated to the completion of

---

[49] Meaning, they get a copy of the finished work to show, credit for their effort on the project and right to show the effort on their resume, etc. and food for being there?

the project's completion or just for this stage? Are you well enough prepared? The Cinema–Libre suggests most things can be done without financial outlay if you have the right equipment present and the right effort from artists with shared goals and views. Obviously also, a script can help.

Manpower: Manpower is a factor of available effort and labor,[50] complicated by outlay to provide human effort. The above factors are meant to avoid waste of such outlay. How many people beyond yourself will you need to accomplish your goal? Why will they be there and what will they need to do? Do they need training or skills? If you, yourself, can advance much of your goals on your own, how much of a commitment of your own time are you needing? Can you be sure even you are available?

Quality: Setting the measure of quality for your own work can be difficult at best. The most prolific writer will not judge his work at completion, other than a sense of completion and joy at the completeness of the work. If you set your goals for quality in terms of sales, you are using an off-track measure. The industry may be less evolved than your work and your genre not sought for years. You also

---

[50] beyond goal-setting labor and into goal-doing labor.

only need to find one buyer, and that person may be decades from you in your life charting. If you are setting goals for quality in terms of length, you may be cheating yourself in terms of brevity and succinity. Set your goals in your writing efforts to the level of achieving the simple feeling you have a product which you as an artist are proud of and you, with effort, will feel you have reached a satisfying level of completeness. Know you, as a writer, will have plenty of time and opportunity for revision if you feel revision is in the best interest of the project. For now, simply advance the words on the page. Consider succicinity. Do you gain more as a writer with embellished, elaborate text or by expressing your goal with immediate directness, clarity and expertise?

Resources: Do you need tools or equipment you don't yet have? Do you need expertise for these types of equipment? Do you need logistics to have the equipment in place? Do you need a place to stage logistics? Do you need permission of some form? Do you need to have copyrights and clearances in order to put forward the work for profit or screening? Do you have insurance in case something goes wrong?

Charter–measure: I state something I learned from the Army in fuller detail in the next chapter. "If a plan is made, a plan is written." A written plan, even for your own work, can be considered a charter-measure. Do you have your goals in writing? Respect your efforts enough to diligently put your goals into fixed form, especially if you are working on the project with another person. If you are going to be working on a project for months or years, you might as well have the goals on paper. Consider Pen, Pencil, and Eraser.

Whether you are working alone or with a partner, give yourself the starting action of creating a Charter–Measure, which sets your goals down. Many examples of these are available in Mark Litwak's Contracts for the Film and Television Industry. Using co-writing agreement charter measure as an example, you may as a writer with a collaborator or co-writer be amiable to setting the agreement itself as both a goal and a measure.

Even setting the agreement to paper will feel both limiting and liberating. Ownership of the project will often be discussed as well as future goals such as assignment of directing responsibility or saleability. Nice to debate these issues before any fights and feelings of investment, even emotional, are on the line compounded with the already real effort. Even the obligations of the writers to each other may be written, such as days a week or hours to invest, or who types the notes.

In completing the agreement you have achieved completion of a goal both writing parties shared and you have completed the measure of the goal in the actual contract. This completed agreement structure provides extra motivation and guidance. You have the tangible measure of the collaboration as per the contract and you will have the requirements of both parties understandable and arranged, and at each step now more competed.

With the co-writer agreement process, at charter measure the written agreement is the goal while the charter measures themselves are functional documents reflecting the agreement. You may even have charter documents which go beyond writing and into co-producing, and position.[51] Most films or plays, by the time they reach production, will have multiple deals in place and anyone who is to receive public credit will have a document to show their participation and role. Remember, similar to *The Social Network,* you may have to release these to have a sale.

Artistic endeavors take effort. A good screenplay is often around 110 pages and has over 130 scenes. Like writing, this

---

[51] I'd again recommend Mark Litwak's book so you aren't starting these agreements from scratch.

much effort on the scale of spending in the production medium is best done at a relaxed, focused pace, and the discipline should carry over to both pre-production and post-production.

At the writing stage, a professional would try to move the pen or cursor at a predictable rate and performance. To be real, keeping your mind on task is sometimes as simple as maintaining in your thoughts the goals, so long as the amalgamate changes. Perusing well-organized ideation tools and adding even small amounts of detail can have tremendous long-term cumulative effect. Often, in storytelling, these little additions can be truly charming and sweet, adding fundamental changes to the overall uniqueness that will have your finished product well received and lovingly remembered.

MEASURES

A goal, when set, will often benefit from a written measure for whether or not the goal is nearing completion, approaching completion, or beyond your current efforts. What is stated as goal is at best produced as measured, or anticipated in planning. Measures are both ways in which efforts are applied and also ways to gauge efforts in their function. [52]

---

[52] In 1997 and 1998 I participated as an actor in a play known as Gunfighter: AGWC (A Gulf War Chronicle) in which I played CWO3 Ross Nettles. I have other training in the field, I am trained on receiving training and wordings, and I even accepted Royal Rifle training as a child, but the preparation for this play was unique. The Army supervised the presentation on uniform and procedures, especially in regards to press and contingency. As a result, I have received and have knowledge of reserve officer training. The training is unique to the individual and tailored to the Army's Intentions.

In the United States Army Reserve Officer Training Curriculum, Effort for Measure is studied, taught and trained. The Army taught me to the point of drilling, if a measure is given a measure, the measure for the measure is, is the measure written in an understandable and doable way? Yes, the Army also teaches and trains measure-completion is a measure of success, and also of goals. This structure is especially involved in the process of planning structure for years, even decades, into the future, with a methodical pace predicted towards the fruition of massive goals, and also at the pace of immediacy of the battle-field.

In the measure for effort, students learn that at the planning stage, planning the goal is the measure. A very well formulated set of steps is presented for the methodical and consistent approach to the completion of goals. You will find they repeatedly explore the question, are you aggressive enough? The training considers this aggression measure "Measure of Aggression" and strongly encourages aggressiveness in final absorption into one plan, with all of the best ideas from smaller plans, to accomplish the most which is accomplishable.

Young officers are encouraged to look at the "whole of the entirety" and to endeavor to create plans which recognize a shifting reality and to create their plans as an improvement to the existing totality which may be both changing and broken into pieces. Sometimes parts and pieces may be used and very, very rarely, an entire plan is put into place.

For training exercise, reserve officers are given real world dilemmas the Army is looking to solve and are asked for solution measures that may be incorporated. The following steps are encouraged to the point of drilling:

Step 1: **Assess the goal's ability or capability**.

The goal sets forward a plan of endeavor. What are you trying to do, learn, create, make etcetera? In other words, what would you like your efforts to manifest? Are you aggressive enough?

Step 2: **Assess the goals**.

With your wording, is the thing doable and explainable? Would someone other than you understand your words? Are you expressing to yourself efficiently what you are trying to accomplish and do? Are you as direct towards accomplishment as you can figure out how to be? Is your aim steady? If the plan is theoretical, how far do you have to deviate from actual successes performed before? Would research benefit your goal? Are you aggressive enough?

Step 3: **Assess the merit**.

Most goals have merit. Is yours well expressed? Are these goals worth risking your time, efforts, and possibly self? Do you assist others with friendly ambitions by accomplishing your goals? Could you be more aggressive?

Step 4: **Assess the cost or risk of cost**.

Could you lose capital? Could you lose reputation? Without well-phrased goals, would you meander aimlessly? What happens if you fail? What is best benefit if you succeed? If your plan is moved forward, are you ready to sacrifice the risk and have you been fully aggressive towards your planned and stated ultimate goals? If the resources are risked and mobilized, have you been aggressive enough in these goals to justify the sacrifice?

Step 5: **Assess the time line**.

Are you hurried? Is there immediate benefit to acting now? Is there liability in waiting? Are you co-operating with others? Do you need to be in sync with them for delivery? Do they have increased risk or liability if you do not deliver immediately or well? Can you get more done to be more ready? Are you aggressive enough?

Step 6: **Assess the cost to merit ratio**.

If funds were unlimited, we could get more done. Funds are never unlimited and planned expenditure benefits from plan-proficiency. Approval is difficult and competing plans will be contemplated. Considering this, are you getting as much done in your plan with any allowed resources as possible? Are the goals you state phrased as understandably and aggressively as possible, considering you may have other people helping you and would like to accomplish as much as possible with any interest or approval given? Are these resources better utilized somewhere else? Why wouldn't you incorporate the best elements of all of these plans?

Step 7: **Assess the lack of time line**.

Do you have any real deadlines? Can these goals be accomplished later, better equipped? Are you too aggressive, meaning aggressive to the point of unnecessary or additional risk? Again, is their increased liability from waiting? Are you aggressive enough?

Step 8: **Assess materials and tools**.

If these goals can be accomplished later, could you be better equipped? Could someone make something custom for you? As a writer, for example, would new tools or software help you more efficiently? If there is great benefit to acting now, do you even have enough tools and resources to move forward to completion? Can you at least advance your goals? Do you know what materials and tools are available in your field and nearby fields? Do you have ample and diverse tools? Are you aggressive enough and is there a chance much better tools will be available with a little money, research or time? Are your current tools good enough for now, especially if any time-power or man-power is already mobilized? Assess. Are you aggressive enough?

Step 9: Begin effort towards the goals.

If your logistics measures have thus far failed, effort towards the goals may mean investing in better tools or training. If your planning measure has failed, you may need to plan anew. If the plan is solid, move the plan to being done. Actualize manpower, meaning get the necessary people in place with the necessary tools actually endeavoring for you. Be aggressive.

You eventually learn the difference between measures and goals are never as clear as at the time of writing, but in their effort stage the difference between goal and measure is nebulous. In effort towards a goal or measure's completion, the effort gets you closer to both goal and measure. I repeat

again, effort gets you closer to both measure and goal.
Before then, to your best endeavor, recognize them as
different or the same. For me, measures are less words and
feelings and are more actionable. When you reach
completion you will then feel your goals and successful
measures are provably the same. This is definably success.

HONEST EXAMPLE

While in film school getting my Masters Degree in the Fine Art of Cinema-Television Production, I had a job working as a post-production monitor for the school. My job was to sit at a desk at entry and make sure the people who weren't supposed to be there couldn't get in, even if desperate, and the people who were supposed to be there had everything they needed. We were still cutting on editing flatbeds at the time and students often needed film splicers, reels for sound and replacement reels if their equipment broke, and sometimes simply honest advice. The students were almost always desperate for time as deadlines neared and I got to know several students at all ranges of stress.

One of the girls in the producing program I had grown to love quite a bit approached me one day beaming with pride. She had an assignment for her writing class to write a scene that could be in a movie. She had written a scene she was very proud of and wanted my opinion. I accepted and as she handed me her scene she began to "justify" the scene. She began to explain other scenes in the movie she hadn't written yet and tried to explain why the punch line was funny. I shushed her, and explained something I had learned when getting my Bachelor's Degree in the Fine Art of Drama. The scene was as ready as the scene.

She began to explain to me she agreed, "But," and then pointed out the scene was part of a whole. I handed her a piece of paper and asked her to show me where in the timeline these scenes were. She graciously acquiesced with a slight curtsey, demonstrated the set-up and punch line with her hand, and let me read the scene. Her written humor was at least amusing, bordering on smiles and charm, but not yet into chuckle. Her unique sense of humor was well presented and captured. Pleased at my pleasure, she somewhat nervously took back the scene and crumpled up the scrap of paper that had freshly held her timeline.

I held her hand as she crumpled the paper and she looked me in the eye, confused as to why I had stopped her in her wrinkle attempt. I wrote an "I" on her scrap of paper, paused for a moment, and changed the line of the "I" to an "A" completing with "Alex thinks you should finish your screenplay."

She looked at the timeline quizzically. "Why'd you make your 'A' that way?" She asked.

I explained, since the comment was for her, I had changed the comment to her point of view. After all, she was the writer.

She looked at her timeline, this time with the eye of a critic. She realized she was further towards her goal than she was when she had simply come to show me her scene. She looked at the scrap of paper quizzically and added more elements to the time line. She looked at me with the smile of a smug little girl, unabashed and unashamed to be smiling. She allowed me to watch her writing and, before my eyes, her story blossomed.

She visited me a few days later, very pleased with her progress. She expressed she wanted to be writing four or five scenes a day and was making great progress. I was happy for her happiness.

She visited me again about two weeks later, now sad. She had slowed in her progress and wasn't making as rapid a progress, "But," she pointed out with a new scene in hand

and a now typed timeline she had made to impress me and also mark her ownership of her concepts, "When I slowed down I wrote another scene which was funny." This scene, in context, was closer to complete.

My job was at a lull and I was still thinking about her. I realized later where she had gone off–track. She had been at the scene level before, and was now trying for a whole screenplay. She was making great progress, but she hadn't yet done scene cards or character cards and was simply writing out of sheer enjoyment and love, without anything but her timeline to guide her. The next time I saw her, I pointed out; all of the scenes she had written on her timeline were written except for one. She, at risk artistically, hostile and defensive, expressed she knew what she wanted to do with that scene. I gently, lovingly suggested she write. I told her I was proud of her for her ambition.

She came back to me four days later again happy. She showed me what had begun to resemble a screenplay. She flipped through the pages of the new scene, seductively denying me a chance to read. I asked why, and she admitted gently that she had a character based on me. Her producing program had taught her how both to be both valued and not sued. I allowed her this gentle admission. I wished her well on her screenplay and told her I look forward to seeing her film someday. She flitted away in bliss.

She poked her head back in a bit later and stated, again selfishly defining ownership, she had not yet shown me her screenplay, only a few scenes. She had my interest. She now had an increasing amount of work to show. She expressed what she was most proud of was her improved timeline. She showed me the bulk of her words and her now more fully-fleshed timeline.

Each scene she had placed on her new, typed, timeline, she had already written, with the exception of one scene she had handwritten onto the timeline on the way to see me. She felt successful. All of the scenes were full and complete, many of them funny. I realized something for both her, and myself, as she stood in front of me, beautiful and pleased with her progress. The organization of the timeline and the gentle encouragement had gotten her to her writing goal, and even further along towards the assignment which she eventually had for the whole semester.

She admitted her fellow students were jealous, still struggling with the same initial assignments, and all of her fellow female students wanted her permission for a moment of my time. I, as per the position, allowed them my time and presence.

Most of the other students who spoke to me needed the same style of help taking the scenes they had written and making them into more developed screenplays. I detailed to them what the first girl had done. They acknowledged her and admitted how much faster than them she was writing. I suggested they emulate her process. Instead of simply writing scenes, I suggested they write a timeline and then write a script, a basic I had heard suggested in my own writing classes but found most amateur writers avoided do to the extra effort. They all endeavored on their own projects to emulate her timeline structure and goals. All found success with the assignment.

At the beginning of their assignment the project seemed surmountable with only consistent effort and talent, but all of the students who put in the effort began to meander without a map. By the time they had written their timelines, they were able to put effort directly to the goals instead of rationalizing the work. All were pleased to have the map to the goals they themselves set. They proved, with a plan, when they were immersed in the ideas, both suggestibility and creativity came more easily.

THE LANGUAGE OF CINEMA

Having spent time amongst the Rieslings, I understand
how important language is to us. The Rieslings are mostly
non-verbal, but they will explain with hands and emotion
what they are feeling, even sometimes giving gifts. The
Rieslings have expressed to me, if humans can do skits for
each other, they can "stop-killing" (A word in their
language suggesting even at the point of fang and fists, killing
can be averted). Something else I learned from the
Monkeys, "Everybody wants to be in skits. If you are going
to be in a skit, be in a good one."

We, as humans, have a different dependence on spoken
language and the specificity words form in our minds. We
need as many words as we have for the complexity and
brevity in our thoughts. The Rieslings, if a human took the

time to talk to them, would eventually gesture to us by indicating to their head that we have too many words. They also, especially to me when I was there, would point to me making a puppet with their hands suggesting I tell the whole world their stories. They often thought of the whole world, which to them meant things beyond Panama as well. The unique geography of the region makes feeling both oceans very easy to do, {and the sunsets spectacular.}

Our language structure took us since the dawn of man to develop. The Language of Math is similar. We see increasing specificity and elegance. Punctuation, for example, was so important a development in language, languages were allowed the very rare allowance to cross-innovate. Normally, most language innovations were kept specific to a language for both military and non-military purposes. With punctuation, languages were able to adapt.[53]

Cinema has grown similarly complex. Each of the methods of expression is specific. A jib isn't a dolly, although it can ride one. A pan isn't a tilt, although they may both occur at the same time with a very skilled operator

---

[53] Italian, for example, innovated the idea of punctuation in Italian, a formal innovation. Spanish, a language I have some familiarity with, also shows the signs of their own innovations. Common usage such as "¿Que Tiempo Hace?" Or "What time do you make?" (Also what tempo, suggesting how fast should we move) shows the elegant use of the Spanish Punctuation, uniquely Spanish.

or very light camera. A crane isn't a carmount, a hostess tray isn't a hood mount on its own, etc. These elegances in the language take years to learn fluently.

The positions in film are similarly specific. Each has their job to do. A Director directs the audience's eyes. He places their viewing onto a specific momentum, including emotion. The director is the most concerned with quality and artistry. A Producer has a job more simply describable as generating the film, in other words at the end of the day, there is a movie. If they are concerned about quality, they are best served to trust their director and give him what he needs to put the movie on the screen, with maybe a few nice embellishments. How do they know what to have there? They trust the script.

I learned the following phrase in my Army Training: "The most important part of Military Legal is Legal." Film legal can be looked at the same way, the same as stated for the military, but most amateurs might not know to agree.

Language is specific and Legal, when real, is written. I know the following from the Rieslings, however: They don't need words to describe their feelings. They describe, "They feel their feelings." I'd like to feel the same. I'd like to live without needing to justify. I'd like to feel my feelings.

My Cinema–Libre tenets, in the first tenet[54], strongly suggest having more than one person putting effort to the film. I learned from Christopher Watts[55] to define myself in a role which can be explained, and to leave the other parts of the filmmaking to the other filmmakers. We agreed to my archaic term "filmmaker" when we were discussing a digital documentary I would still love to make called "Prayer Call." Prayer Call is a jail documentary about the men in Twin Towers who are awaiting trial and pray.

Christopher's advice is well taken and I would give young filmmakers the same advice. "Put yourself forward on each film as the servant in the role." Ultimately, our shared goal is the ultimate movie. I added these: Moving, Picture, Sound, emotion.

Interesting, at least to me, a writer in the digital age most likely no longer moves a physical pen. In the Cinema–Libre,

---

[54]The First Tenet of Cinema-Libre States: To the Cinema-Libre Filmmaker, money does not exist. Cinema-Libre is an expression of pure creativity, free of fears of profitability and commerciality. All filmmakers and films working under the Cinema-Libre Code should recognize the divine state of being and that state's innate ability to create everything from nothing. In this creator's image, all skills, materials, talent, lighting elements, design elements, production equipment and other tools must be native to the artists, borrowed from friends or liberated. Manual labor and other working as a bartering tool is strongly encouraged as the Cinema-Libre Filmmaker is expected to be of service.

[55] the inspiration behind the Christopher Society whose famous motto "Better to light a candle than curse the dark,"

however, I am trying to bring us back to this primal order. As noted, I also use the somewhat archaic in a modern digital era term, filmmaker, although increasingly no acetate is purchased.

As a filmmaker, I have a fair and honest approach to how I schedule my crew. Writing is guide, enacting is essential, time is valuable and people are key. I have had, on a small scale, a lot of luck scheduling a $2/3^{rds}$ day with my crew and motivating first shot with the stated goal, make my shot, make, my day, make my movie. I do small storyboards and disperse them easily, often thirty or more on a single 8½ by 14. If we get done on time, we get better coverage. Even the crew gets to get more aggressive in camera coverage and shots. One crewman pointed out we wouldn't have a problem keeping them if we were for ensample, "still tipping," meaning like-a-waiter, putting money in their pockets.[56]

---

[56] As traditional, I normally shrug, and point out openly; to the filmmaker money does not exist.

REVISIONS

One of my first guild level jobs in Hollywood was as a Writer's Assistant for a WGA Writer, Sue Black. My job was to take the notes she and the producer were giving and to put them into the electronic version of the script on Final Draft. The job is specialized and was a great job for me during film school as I was not only learning and working on real projects, I was able to apply the actual professional formatting to my own assignments for my screenwriting classes. I learned a lot.

The most often asked questions for me regarding this type of expertise in the ideation process regard how to deal with the overwhelming prospect of revisions and drafts. The first deals with order of operations. If you have massive changes,

I highly recommend doing structural changes first such as re-ordering chapters, and then using the word-processor's "Find" function to find the spot you are applying the note. Especially if you are combining information from different parts of my main structure, you will have a much more realistic effort in combining the pieces into a coherent whole.

As a writer, I feel I benefit to remember both you the audience, and I, the filmmaker have goals, and also my characters have goals. Well-set goals can make the difference between aimless meandering and complete productivity. Too many young filmmakers write about a filmmaker. I find them artistically young. After all, in theater, not every play is "A Chorus Line." There are the occasional genius efforts, but they are few and far between for their plentiful presentation.

The other film genre rampant in my tire of film school involved writers writing about writer's block. Often, they misperceived deadlines and misperceived their own struggle and cinematic worthiness. Why waste the opportunities of film school there? I'd ask them to consider something I delve into more later in asking myself, "What is moving in the frame? How are my characters afraid for their lives? What do they risk? How do they fight?

When a person is immersed in ideas, both suggestibility and creativity are more accessible and the corrections come more easily. Sometimes measure can go beyond goal if the goals are well set, for example if you feel complete to fill a whole page and end up getting more done in the same space for effort. Meeting quota on goal is often being able to add new goals to a current set of goals which neither conflict nor deter.

WHEN THEY SEE YOUR WORK

We don't often make the same mistakes, twice. At the very least, we don't often make the same bad mistakes all-the-way twice. I know that as I get a little older, my issue isn't so much a constant fear of my end. I am able to enjoy more the actual useful effort increasingly avoid what is even feeling unpleasant in my efforts and endeavor. One thing that is unpleasant which I avoid is total failure. Another is total stagnancy.

As I have worked professionally in post-production, I have seen the radical differences between Feature Films and the aim of Feature Film Perfection compared with Broadcast Television and the constant need to feed the beast of time-slot and audience expectations of new material. As digital film begins to give real options in cost-reduction and

savings, I am not interested in only looking a question I am
trained to often face in army-logistics of "Can we eliminate
this to save money?" In Feature Film, as example, the art of
editing online[57] vs. editing offline;[58] at this stage of
progression and growth, I am not interested in eliminating
the labor, and therefore cost, of online. While the quality of
the offline footage is increasing, I do not see the elimination
of the care-level devoted at online. I am more interested in
seeing the improvement of quality this laborious stage can
create. Old chemical process film used both, and I am insist
on the quality which results from respecting both processes
as separate, and not worth the few thousands to combine. I
feel sophisticated as an artist to both endure labor and to
avoid foulness and repulsiveness. Online is clean. I at least
insist my films be marketable and ready for the world to
consume.

As a filmmaker, with nod to documentary realism, we, in
the world, recognize and grow from the exploration of
ourselves and others in what is now greater in valor as

---

[57] old fashioned for one-to-one, meaning your media is complete and forward and theoretically in the old days especially at risk

[58] my specialty at Vision Quest Entertainment, where a lower resolution, lower cost version is physically or digitally manipulated artistically to compose the basic elements of the image and sound

example. Film is the most complex, active medium of story and we have responsibility to accurate depiction and honest evaluation of every element put before camera and shown with our power to the world.

If you create work and the world, in your honest feelings and soul expression, does need your giving and is not yet ready for your voice, do the work.

One of the things Frank taught me, at least on Master Contract, you only let a contractor off on a finished product. If you order a hamburger with pepperjack cheese and the think comes back with cheddar, you send that burger back right away or accept you have cheddar cheese.

Put in the time to your society to allow those around you, like an army, to feel, to believe, and to grow ready for your giving. Even if you need to start the effort again, you will be granting to all what you are: Artist and Provocateur.

THE NITTY-GRITTY

With the size of the professional job sometimes being apartment complexes, which covered acres, when I was working with Frank, we would often paint in the same color for five days straight. A very large apartment complex might get painted once every five years, and requires twenty men to prep and paint. Awnings and trim were extra, and Fine Line's decorating specialty.

If the brushes and rollers were going to be used with the same color paint the next day, they didn't require the same amount of massive diligence. We got more wall covered and less delays, from the group of us sticking to the task and letting some paint stick to the brushes. With a higher level of skill, we didn't sacrifice any quality as the paint wouldn't run. We also didn't have the paint rip-up when the tape would have been removed. This level of expertise is expert down to the nitty-gritty.

At the beginning of this ideation process, you will feel like you have little scraps of ideas. Eventually, your work will be filled enough to reach the casual, first-time reader. This level of development is fun to do, if you are well suited to the artistry.

In this process, some artists are chaotic, they frantically shape and chisel their concepts. Others are orderly; they apply concept after concept in a logical order. The tools should serve both factions. Remember, while working on problem areas, you are working on what is broken, non-functional, or problematic. In surgery, you are safer to remove them, but what do you lose? If you try to spread them around to save your investment, you are poisoning what is healthy. A master's touch is required.

As a writer, contemplating and expressing your ideas at least to yourself is the first step. The first step can be the easiest and you have several opportunities for several types of first steps such as first steps delving into a character, and first steps delving into a scene. In contemplation, better reasoning normally means a better scene erupts.[59]

---

[59] I like reasoning out-loud before I write, as I feel gain with less-inefficiency in my written statements towards the project.

If you are writing, explore in the safety and privacy of your own journals. These skills are useful for anyone, even someone trying to write for reasons other than their own development as a professional.[60] Begin to allow the rawest inklings to grow as the set of tools maintains your forward progress. You can experiment with the tools, both story and ideation, which you have available. At the barest level, even a memo pad may suffice. Explore your story tools. Imagine a character that either teaches or observes the growth the heroes go through. How old is the character? What motivates the character? Why does the character take such interest? Write two scenes at different points of the hero's knowledge. Remember that they do not need to be sequential.

By the time you go through the process of placing all of your ideas into the medium of your endeavor closest to the audience,[61] you will feel you have earned the sense of completeness for completion. I love this feeling as I feel like the project I have worked on is the project I have made. Your book, or screenplay, or even finished edit will resonate with the well–used ideas you have shepherded.

---

[60] Many discover the catharsis of writing and find the effort similar to an expertise I have of drama-therapy.

[61] For the Screenwriter, the Screenplay. For the Editor, the Edit, etc.

Fundamental morality is a concept in writing. Have your characters deal with interesting moral challenges. As you imagine your main characters instead of the traditional in Hollywood question, "What is the character's fatal flaw?" consider of your characters that they may have more than one thing they struggle against. Consider granting them one or more of the seven deadly sins: Pride, Lust, Avarice, Greed, Wrath, Envy and Sloth. Give them as many as you feel are best representative of your story goals and consider then filling in for the characters any or all of their antithesis the seven valorous virtues: chastity, temperance, charity, diligence, patience, kindness, and humility.

Has this process taken months to this level of complexity? Have you worked with a partner for those months? You can now leave the nest and venture beyond safe ground. Feel proud you work can stand on it's own. Even as an audience member, be prepared to join a larger movement,

SITE SAFETY

As a writer or any other type of artist, allow yourself the luxury of creating as fostering an environment as you and your resources can muster. Consider your surroundings and the people around you and contemplate who is a good person if any for you to show your infant work.

I have learned with tools especially, PRIORITIZE SAFETY. Safety can include working at a steady pace and towards a predictable schedule. Look to your own situation. Can your calendar stay safe for your project for a whole year? If yes or no, are creativity appointments, other functions and artist's dates worth scheduling? Give yourself room to go through the initial frustrations and disappointments.

Continue your efforts. Make yourself protected by knowing the following concepts of who is in your welcome-tier:

Are you safe?
Are you comfortable?
Are your ideas safe enough to share?
Do you trust your compatriots?
Do you sense any danger?
Can you discuss titillation?

Setting safe spaces for you can be a measure for success. You should always maintain physical safety. Don't push measures of fatigue and be open to leaving your ideas and tools in place if you are not safe. Seek safety immediately. As a writer you may need to also maintain emotional safety, emotional safety space, and safety for your ideas.

Safety counts, and eventually contributes to the bottom line. As Dean of the College of Cinema-Arts at the University of Southern California, Elizabeth Daley taught us "Every rule in Hollywood is written in blood." She meant, someone got hurt to make the profiteers make a rule to protect people.

One of the most frustrating things for a writer in terms of shifted progress and goal is not having the safety and space to enjoy and reflect upon your ideas. People not involved in

101

direct participation with the project will often take offense to you suggesting they are somehow hurting your goals through their normal activity and communication and often most aggressively, their curiosity or even admiration. Remember your goals and measure your success. Do you owe your project you may have more safety? Do you owe yourself the chaos for an artist of an interruptible art–space? What honestly gets you closer to your goals? What means do you have available? Are your available means shifting your actuactable goals?

If you are writing, consider yourself a writer. A likeable and polite behavior can be to give fellow writers the same respect. At the beginning of collaboration, be aware of others' hyper-defensive state. They may attempt to protect themselves from judgement at the sacrifice of stated goals. For the first few weeks, they may be shy, reticent or possibly even wanting to make fun of the process. Some may be so defensive, they will put forward they are too cool to be there, but bothered to show up.

Social structure is something that needs to be learned. Rules and structure often go beyond simple observation. You and your fellow artists will need to set discipline where you will feel safe to be around each other and vulnerable as you offer up fledgling ideas. Even beyond the charter-measure, be sensitive to co-writer's social circumstances. As you gain momentum, also give yourself the luxury of these continued concepts of safety in ideation:

Do you have an audio safe environment?

Can you for example, enact dialogue?

Can you reason outloud?

Are you safe enough to have emotion?

Does your environment limit your abilities to laugh?

Do you have space enough to cry?

Are you safe to admire progress?

Do you need someone to show your work?

Even supportive people commenting on liking hearing you typing or laughing can make you self-conscious, which can make you slow or alter your work. Go back to basics. Return to your tools and their basic functions.

In an artistically questionably safe environment, there is even more value to having your ideas well stored and well written. If, for example, an artistic environment becomes unsafe, you may return to your well-stored tools and the concepts on them and you may restart without much loss. To whatever extent you have filled in your work, you still have the same level of scenes, characters, and basic sense of structure. If you return to your work, at least you will not have lost progress. Continue from where you are and you will eventually be able to show you have put these ideas together.

Upon reaching artistic safety, celebrate what makes you unique. Celebrate the uniqueness of people you love. Be honest, in both your work and your life and enjoy the success–ability you have endured to hold. If there is a fight, reconcile. In this, be a professional as Frank Barnes taught me. He said, "One of the main differences about being a professional is not making mistakes. Another main one is knowing how to fix them."

As you mature, let your deadlines be safe spaces, too. Keep them self–imposed at least until people are offering you actual capital. If you are working with a partner, set small deadlines for just you and them, no one else needs to be involved. What is an example of a small deadline? Anything that makes you feel the need to push for completion. Move forward your tangible goals. Keep your progress clean and memorable. Motivate the more passive ideas to at least stand up enough to be formed into words.

As a young contractor, Frank pointed out to me I would tell people my ideas before I had done them. He stated, "If you are proven correct you will have done so." See through what you set out to do.

Learn to give yourself a place safe enough to be free of distractions. Creating a safe space to work also includes that you should be allowed your goal level of concentration. If, for example, you get into a groove and then find yourself subjected to frustrating circumstances, you can feel as though you are as blocked as when you feel the absence of suggestibility. Sometimes, people who are not involved in the process do not give you space to not include them. They feel their interest in your process is more important than your feelings towards the material and your growth. They do not understand you are a writer, and most likely have never written. Choose deliberately to either include them or not, and consider changing locale if you are mobile so as to not offend your local circle of loved ones who may mean the best of intentions but do not actually help you towards your tangible goals.

Dirty looks can kill progress. Do not allow yourself to fail simply because someone else is jealous or snooping. I can understand why so many writers are believed to find isolated cabins to complete their work. Free yourself of any frustrating obstacles. Do not be angry. Feeling unsafe can spoil growth.

If you are so reliant, in a modern mobile era, on a perception of sameness and normalcy creating stagnancy, you have no one but yourself to blame for repeated interruptions in the immediacy of the expression of suggestible creation. As Eckhart Tolle states in The Power of Now, "If you do not like your life situation, change it."

If a person or people are willing to intentionally invade your safe-space with any intent deviant to your goals, consider them hostile, but do not let them block your progress to your measures of your goals. Bolster your defenses and also your deliberateness to put effort towards your defense. Be less showing to them of the work you have done and do not give them enough to even critique your efforts in progress. Do not allow them derail you or to escalate in anger. In place, be calm and productive.

DEEP SUGGESTION AND CHAOS

When you begin to work with the tools, allow the semi-blank page to be inviting. If you are excited to be writing and ideas are just beginning to flow, gently go over the concepts the ideation tools present. They should also be exciting to begin to contemplate and inspiration should be easy.

I believe in deep suggestion. Ideation tools can help a deep suggestion state to more efficiently get the artist as vessel to the development level of artist toting completed work. Deep Suggestion is a state of awareness in which the subconscious mind is activated in a way where the depth of thought is to the core of the psyche's connection to that which is beyond the psyche. The conscious thought pattern, which is often riddled with self-criticism and doubt, is wrested aside and the part of the creator that is able to connect to the essence of creation is able to create without dilemma. The human mind is designed to forget dreams, so as to not confuse reality. We are, even in our subconscious while dreaming, connected to the Zeitgeist. Images and remembrances in our dreams connect to things in our minds, even those things we have offset from our conscious delving. Things in our imagery, even in dreams, are connected to things larger than ourselves.

If you find yourself literally dreaming of your project or even just your characters, don't waste your creativity and impressionability. Work to be sentient enough to physically at least write your ideas onto the chicken scratch at the minimum. Have tools at your bedside so they may be able to remember what your conscious mind may forget. Above all, find the tools useful. You will eventually again sleep and be rested, press to the pad and write.

Feel safe with the tools you have and, as with any tool, grow increasingly proficient with them as you increase what you know. If you are confident in what the tool is used for, use the tool with confidence. If you don't know what the tool is used for, there may be a better tool that is simpler and less confusing. Peruse the tools.

Begin to experiment with the tools you have. To begin to try the tools, start with pencil on the character and scene tools. Gently escalate to pen. As ideas begin to form regarding things beyond simple scenes and characters, advance to pencil on the project journals. Again, advance to pen. When these ideas being put into your project journal begin to take shape in words as fundamental to the overall project, put the ideas into your prized idea journals as a safe-keep memento holder and know you are one step shy of beginning your project in earnest in the form you set as goal to completion: your play, your screenplay, your novel, or your song. Even jotted, to the extent your ideas are stated, your expression exists.

WRITING TOOLS

In ideation, the active process of coming up with ideas, if one is able to trust ideation tools to hold ideas, is one safe enough ease mental burden? Ideation can be learned. Can you relax as you can comfortably forget previous ideas? In such a place, a person may return to the ideas again to refresh themselves repeatedly. When one views the ideas again and even makes radical changes with the safety of the thoughts in place, a person can make radical growth if something unanticipated or new arises in their thought process. They can safely return to them newly inspired, even re-inspired by what they have on the page, allowing each re-visitation to bring them closer and closer to their goal or goals.

If you are a writer, with this book, I am endeavoring to not only help you to be an artist, but to be a predictable artist who can sit down and make predictable progress at nearly every writing opportunity.[62]

What is the difference between a predictable artist and a professional artist? Whether or not he or she gets paid. In the Cinema-Libre, we do not try to avoid getting paid, we try to avoid having lack be an obstacle. We are not downtrodden.[63] In my own professional time in the industry, at first, people felt lucky to get paid. I have learned, "Luck meets endeavor." Often, writers sell more than one project at a meeting if they're prepared. I encourage you to endeavor to take the advice of Julia Cameron in The Artist's Way: You worry about the quantity, let God worry about the quality.

At the goal-setting stage, what would you like to have in the story at completion for both you and for your project?

---

[62] While getting my BFA, one of my acting professors, Susan Shaugnessy stated to another actor who was nervous, "I don't need you to explain your scene, I need you to perform your seen so I can grade you."

[63] Regarding our Cinema-Libre, my beloved Justice DiLaurentiis, future executive producer of many of my films and daughter of recently deceased and famed producer Dino DiLaurentiis, suggested in talking to "A-Grade Talent" who often have their salaries set, they may be told, "You get what you make." In the reality of what is what, we all make what we make. She also refuses to feel downtrodden, even by my ethos, mythos, logos, and pathos. For all four, I feel of myself is this work and effort I can be proud of? I am proud of her for being genuinely supportive of me with what she knows and has.

Have you emphasized these things in the body of the expression? For me, as an example, the Cinema–Libre Tenets are meant to be embodied, beyond emulated. Also, for me as an artist the Cinema–Libre Tenets being used by other artists are a goal of mine, and I would like to see others choose to use what I have put forwards in their own artistic endeavors.

The measure for effort is the Tenets being enacted and present in my culminative work. My own personal goals are defined. Mine took years for me to develop and accept. Do you have a similar for yourself to help you craft a career of projects? If so, consider them tools and get to work. If you are still finding your own morality, make bold enough choices and begin the process of finding your own way.

THINKING ALLOWED

As an artist and a man, I know my hands are cleaner than my feet. That which I trudge through is filthier than that which I do.

A question often asked of me is, "Why are you allowed to do things others are not?"

My answer to them is, "I have learned to do them in a way which is legal. I understand, 'Why we fight.' I also understand clear and primal rights. I have been taught and trained legal wordings. I have understood teaching and training to the point I have defined Training as: The thing has happened so many times, thought process can occur."

They ask, "Why can't I divulge my training?"

I respond, "Your training is still secret and part of a group. I am Army of One."

People who aren't what they claim and aren't concerned with legal-first don't comply. Those people eventually get into a lot of trouble. Feeling powerful and being powerful aren't the same thing. Feeling healthy and being healthy aren't the same thing, either.

People who have put effort forward their whole lives, unconcerned with the rules, have never put their focus to the order and discipline of society. We all fit into a larger circle. Some, in that circle, are able to do things for the whole, where others stop those who would simply seek to disrupt or destroy.

My film movement is an example of not only the self-operation expected of me[64] and the sheer audacity militarily and propagandically demanded of me. The movement is growing. I got an early copy of this book to my friend and cleric, Jihad Turk, who gave me my first Qur'raan. Jihad got the hardcover version to the Muslim Council of Nations. I am the first external propaganda movement accepted by them to their nation, especially with the invitance for debate.

The Muslims and Muslim Nations, for national and theatrical film release, sought morality and Muslim ideals.

---

[64] Notice I still am allowed a team.

They also wanted space to debate. I introduced to them my film movement, and I am very proud to admit we are the first movement to be approved by the Muslim Council. With their approval, we are now allowed to be accepted in each nation on a nation-by-nation and film-by-film basis.

It is my understanding we can show the script scan created through our software, and then each nation may debate with the comparison of this information and the finished film, and decide are we theatrical release, government release, or restricted? We look forward to their films as well and do hope all of the participating nations, including the United States, receive and give the promised minimum of Sixteen Screens.

We hope to gently introduce into their theater our propaganda as well, similar to what we have seen success with in Asia. There, in Asia, they still love John Wayne. I appreciate him also.

While the Muslims and others have shown their fortitude, we can look globally at near-history. In Asian nations, through direct influence, we have grown more enviable and acceptable. Nations who have put forward Morals and Religion first have made our propaganda release stymied. Considering our recent war structure, I consider these issues military. This movement and book is a military act of compassion as we have killed many recently in intrusion.

The United States has long thrived on cultural sincerity. To battle an enemy who strived to "Kill the Great Satan," we need to manifest our good. The enemy can become friends. Claracy and chaplaincy are not the same thing. I am not a chaplain. I offer claracy. In Chaplaincy they try, without judgement to administer God. I define God as "All that is and ever will be." I note slyly as a Christian, he often has a sense of humor. He has self-defined to me as "The Biggest."

As Claracy, I try to be as understandable as possible. In order to maintain cultural coherence, we need morality in our media, in all forms, even pornography (if made), and we absolutely must penetrate all global markets.

Acceptance in Muslim Theatre sounded difficult, but they never discouraged me from aiming high, for example believing in a branch space program and also finding my own path with religious claracy. While complying to Hearts and Minds Campaign Goals, we now go beyond simple admission and into formal propaganda. The Muslims pointed out, they have not yet needed to approve a film to accept the rules. They are content to allow rules before cinema.

116

I have learned as a Muslim, follow the rules, and work to know them. The rules apply to everyone, especially the larger the rule set. People of service do not have separate rules, nor do judges or moguls. Cheating is punished, conscientiousness is rewarded, and the world is watching.

Do not hurt others without reason to hurt others. Do have feelings and efforts of good will towards people who have effort and feelings of good will. Do not start trouble without expecting trouble. Expect people to defend themselves. Do not attack without regard for their defense. Attack only with reason and altruism, and do not allow unmitigated selfishness to goal.

HAPPY ENDEAVOR

Since a person cannot assess quantity and quality by the same gauge, a reasonable fulfillment for you as a writer is being happy with your level of endeavor towards your intentions. You obviously still have a life to live.

You do not need to upset the life you enjoy. You will be more likely to finish your objective measure if you do not find most of your idea creating to be a labor or a task to endure. You will find moments of your effort to be choresome, but the feeling shouldn't ever dominate your life.

As you grow as a writer, set aside three or four years to not set aside three or four years. Do other things, beyond your projects. Your experiences will make you grow and if

you grow as a person, you will grow as an artist as well.
What you learn you can give. In the process, refer to your
tools often.

Let writing be unobtrusive and a steady effort. When
you sit down at your computer to write and are simply
staring at a blank page, if you have a blank page and
notecards, at least you have notecards. There is so much
open territory on the blank page, if you don't have any
structure coming in you will simply meander.

Value even small amounts of progress so long as the
progress is real. The amount of effort to craft a well-worded
novel, screenplay, or epic poem clearly requires months of
labor. Songs are at least a day. Stay encouraged and know
the project is closer to complete with more thought process,
regardless of time spent on the project or time away from the
project since your last delving. For example, you sit down
to write and fill a page in your project journal or complete
an excellent paragraph. You may have simply sat down to
write, but you met the action of completion to at least have
moved your project forward. Those words aren't going
away. An experienced professional may also then advance
the ideas to being in the project binder, on scene or
character cards or character relationship workbooks, or into

the finished screenplay, etc. thus cleaning the initial ideation tools and preparing them for their next use.

Baby progress markers should be validated. Two opposing examples are you have reached a point of completion to the point you can rest or you have reached a point of inspiration where setting your project aside is nearly agonizing. Set aside the electronic tools for a moment and begin to delve into major points again with pen and paper. Can you imagine whole new scenes at these points, again using screenwriting as an example? If you are content, can you endeavor towards your prized idea journal, perhaps with pencil?

When your tools become overwhelming in the cleaning process, since each is a little chaotic and sullied with the pieces of your thoughts they contain, be methodical in the cleaning. Clean and ready your tools. When your ideas are in the binder, on, for example, well filled character or scene cards, or into your screenplay in finished screenplay form, then you can consider the idea completed and the ideation tool clean as well. Be content to rest, then, for now.

As you mature, above all continue writing. Take a breath. Be sure to respect your accomplishments. You have enough dry ink on your pads and notecards, etceteras, to feel backed up. Did you imagine this point at the initiation of your project? Be unattached to the perceived burden that was incomprehensible to writers who have never reached this level of development or contemplated ideation tools. You are, essentially, far enough into your goal to feel content, for the now. Do not be overwhelmed in the now. Again, take a deep breath. Your ideas are safe and as secure as your journals, and as developed as well as your written thoughts.

CARING FOR YOURSELF

Writing works of length can take considerable time and the amount of concentration over that time is something to consider. Focus on your ideas too intently and they will not benefit from major change. Be too far from them and they will not evolve at all. The more you delve into your goals, the more they will progress.

In the presence of endeavor, move forward your goals. Learn to embrace all things present, even fatigue and sleeplessness and let all things present guide you to the effort and the tools. Respond to your body as your sleep cycle changes and be kind to your body if you encounter a greater demand for nutrition.

Know that not everyone around you is a writer and you do not need to explain your artistry to people who are unsafe until your work is developed enough to withstand criticism on the work's own merit. Almost anything of covetable or enviable value I have ever had came from people betting against me. Can you use the inevitable obstructions to allow you to assess your project, and, like a sculptor begin shaping a different part of the same whole? Most likely the ideas will still be around and will still be as manifest when you return to the same detail work in the future at a less frustrated space.

Your cooperative systems should and will increasingly allow you space to create.   Remember space is both a physical and chronological thing.   Time in your day and space physically are both necessary. If you find your once messy desk is now clean and inviting, etc., recognize your growth and show self-appreciation. In Feng Shui, you have reduced the chaos in your life by reducing the clutter on your desk. If you realize for whatever reason, at whatever depth of your psyche, you needed to create a barrier against interruption, again be kind to yourself and your goals. Try, especially if your own barrier is in the way, to soften your barrier and increase your defense. Remember, however, your goal isn't to gain allies against others who you may have perceived as hostile. Your goal is to create.

Setting Goals is important; but accurately measuring your progress and your set-intent is something most people have great difficulty with separate from goal. Successful people do not have this dilemma. For example, they would like to run a mile in less than five minutes. This is both a goal and a measure. They would like to leg-press 280, both a goal and a measure. They would like to make a million dollars, again both a goal and a measure. Easy to put effort and effort-improvement towards.

The more specific the goal, the more functional the goal as a measure. Looking again at the exercise model, a better goal may be completing sets of ten at a weight today as this example of a goal may be more efficient than a long term goal unreachable today. Regularity benefits all things. Consistency breeds measure for the goal. Specificity, as demonstrated in the nutrition objective of using food as a building block after a workout, instead of simply eating whatever is appetizing and saying to yourself, "I've earned this meal" is another good goal objective. As a healthy person, you may succeed more with the nutrition statement, "I have this body goal." You may even have additional goals such as to lower blood sugar, decrease sugar response time, and strengthen your body or lower overall calorie intake. These types of specific goals become more useful all the way from food purchase to food preparation and enjoyment.

Discipline extends beyond food. For Example, if you drink are Bloody Mary's better than shots? Are Starbucks VIA Ready Brew Lattes better then shots? Is a work wine what you're wanting? Is sobriety?

Too much of anything can be a productivity killer. Be the proper grown-up. Consider others. Polish friends taught me to buy potato Vodka and chill my vodka[65]. If you choose to drink, be doing good drinking. "It's the best." There are a lot of people sitting on their goals. This isn't the same as resting on your laurels.

Beyond booze, look at your other patterns. Is Olive Oil better than Canola? In place of mindless embibement, can you do something fun from your childhood, for example, "I like square cut Pizza?"

Writing takes time. The better writers learn to love themselves, long term. In my experience, there are two types of writers. There is the professional model that would write 1,000 screenplays if they had 1,000 ideas of their own. The other, normally from wealthy parents, has set out to write one screenplay, normally described in the first person by them as "my screenplay." They have often moved to a

---

[65] Literally set your Vodka to the freezer until frost sets on the bottle in normal atmosphere. Otherwise you have not lived life, and you rush to drink.

major writing center like New York, or Los Angeles and are genuinely pursuing their dream of writing their screenplay. I consider both models valid, and I like talking to both of them. Whichever of these camps you fit into, know in moving your concepts, you have at least advanced your measures and your goals.

A person in the professional model, prolific or otherwise, is often trying to sell his or her screenplay. Note at their goal structuring and formation, the goal is fairly nebulous. Who, why, how aren't set. In terms of "writing on spec," or speculation writing (meaning no one has paid you for my effort or product), obviously selling a product is easier when you have one to sell. If you are trying to advance as a writer, identify in yourself, are you doing more to add to the words on the page, or more to any other effort while still describing yourself as a writer? The Writers Guild of America uses, "How many of the words were written by each writer" to determine ownership. How are you moving along?

THE EFFORT AHEAD

The further you are from your ideas, the more the ideas will sort of just float around in the back of your head. There is nothing negative about this so long as the ideas are not simply forgotten. Be willing to delve into your tools at differing points in order to keep your own interest sufficient. Going over works you have left mostly developed; you will invariably see things you would like to change.

When you are immersed in an idea, both suggestibility and creativity are more accessible and the connections come more easily. What do I mean by connections? The major union of ideas into form. Essentially, the evolutions of thoughts into manifest writing so long as you actually move the pen, pencil, or cursor.

Critics may doubt, even you may have fears of quality, but ultimately as an artist, your greatest accomplishment is the immutability of the work on the page expressing what you set out to say. The work is, when complete, as rewarding as the time and the effort could be. With concepts in motion like setting a goal to complete a screenplay in a year, you do have something to show for your effort come the project completion, greater in merit than the achievement of the goal in time gauge.

Anything in the future is a fleeting projection. Anything in the past, left unfulfilled, is a phantom. What are real for you as a writer are the words on the page, the blanks left better marked in, and the fruition of the final form. Sublime, complete, unwavering in their reality, unthreatenable in their presentability your final concept in casting of the word is unquestionable to anyone. You are the writer.

In the I Ching, an ancient text from China, a man is suggested to be better by having a child, writing a book, and planting a tree. To the Chinese proverb example, you are one step closer to having a child, writing a book, and planting a tree by doing so.

The quality of your project's reception has only to do with the quality of goal you set as an artist for yourself and the attainment of the realization you set forward. Be Real. As a writer, prove yourself such by writing. Allow your goals to reside within you. Know as a writer, you have too much to do and you have nothing to do in the meantime. If you value the quality of your final effort, add to the character inter-relationship and know, by doing so, you have furthered your character driven drama. Take a breath to imagine your characters fondly. Be content.

Screenplays and novels on a basic level are nothing more than words on a page. Those words, well-inspired, need structure and guidance and effort, nothing more. As storytellers, characters are tools for a writer. Well-crafted characters and scenes are as much tools for writers as words. Even in a story without language such as Masque work and modern dance, you would still present characters in a setting or at least characters as archetypes. Learn to show your story.

Ideation tools, properly seasoned, can help to hone past productive frustration. The seemingly insurmountable dilemma of forming unfathomed ideas now has a body and form. In your polished product, nothing needs to be explained beyond what the finished play, screenplay, etc offers. The finished work is complete enough on its own. In the interim, ideation tools, well created in a system, can alleviate the frustration of ideation while aiding the productivity. We may use ideation tools to channel our ideas from scratch and structure. For these tools, structure is the fundamental of completion and completion is the goal.

As a writer, there are some steps that are repetitive and are often steps you need to get done. Good ideation tools help you to focus on getting words on the page while assisting you in organization and order. Unobnoxiously, they can be forceful reminders of what elements you have not yet filled in with their blank sections reminding you, you can do more.

Ideation Tools can be a great help towards giving you a structure and a format. Structure and format have benefits at different levels of professionalism and engagement. With well-used tools, there is already a discipline to the structure of the tools. Part of the discipline is reaching for the tool when the idea is there.

This tendency will take you all the way to completing the final screenplay, although you needn't be concerned about this at the first week of writing if you are using the tools and the system of tools well. Realize, in this example where you are using the tools, when you are holding the discipline of just writing scene and character cards which can still be moved around easily, you may not be writing a screenplay, but you are writing a movie. Each character and scene will have you one step closer to the goal.

You may discover other things in your life have taken your attention and you, upon returning to the writing, find your process enjoyably more advanced than you remembered. Leaving things in place is a great technique for advancing goal. Ideation tools help this greatly as the ideas progress forward, but the old tools with the rawer ideas in place can stay the same.

You can refer back to the tools for your initial inspiration. If you discover you had made more progress than you remembered, thank the tools and yourself for using the tools for holding more than your own memory by writing and pushing the actualizing of fulfillment of your story closer to the now. Move forwards the ideas on the tools.

For your own benefit, never forget developing your ideas at the basic stage of outlining and scene cards as you determine structure before you find yourself entrenched in the fine details of dialogue and writing physical exchange in the more finished script. Ideation tools grant raw ideas structure, to help raw ideas evolve to a more finished form. Remember, scenes can and should be movable in relationship to each other. If you have an idea, get the idea to a scene card. Make your effort with the largest goal in sight.

As a gifted human, all things we touch and make tangible are tools if guided to creation. The more elegant the tool system, the more elegant a creation can be made. Tools in the hands of an expert craftsman each have a design function and in the realm of the filmmaker, tools will help any filmmaker to fill in the areas of their artistry more fully and with more intricate individuality, thus making each story more socially pertinent, useful as a teaching tool, fun and inspired. As humans, we have a tendency to put order to anything we put effort. We have been granted gifted guided hands.

OUR ERA DEFINED

We live when even the selection of available media is cacophony. Modern media vending provides us nearly endless entertainment options. We choose to "stream" entertainment more often, and as stated before, choose directly what we receive. As we choose what we receive, we choose what we, in our own person, emulate and how we accord through example.

As our storytelling takes on forms of motion and sound, so too may our ideas and tools. We now record thoughts as sound recordings and have digital imaging of everything from family gatherings to fantastic sunsets. These tools may also help the writer, the poet, the playwright, the filmmaker, and the songwriter, if well used. We learn as we grow. People still want to tell their story.

I remember when wired phone line modems were 14.4
kbs. It took forever to download 60 mb and while my Zip
disk could hold them, most files would fracture before
receipt. We invented Cloud Swarming and now enjoy 60
mb downloads in 8 seconds with no fracture evidence. My
cell phone in film school had a 14.4 kbs modem and we are
now to dsl speeds with the multi-generational such as 5g.
We now wonder, with advances in Wi-Fi and Bluetooth,
are they faster, or is plugging in a cable.[66]

Digital gives new options. I would like the films of
Cinema-Libre to maintain Box Office once we are done
filmmaking, in efforts to retain royalty. The next fourteen
years we have premium service ie. Netflix interspersed with
cable channels who provide premium service making back
their investment on product and investment on delivery
structure. My eventual goal in The Cinema-Libre is we,
counting DVD and extra features, are making movies where
the whole of the cinema experience is cinema du reél. As
for the other side of free, at least in participating nations, free
for all after ten years of recoup through box, DVD, and Pay

---

[66] On the military side-of-things, My predecessor's predecessor, a Great War Veteran thought "almost
immediately" meant twelve hours. My predecessor a Korean War, Vietnam and Storm/Shield
Veteran felt "almost immediately" meant twelve minutes. I believe "almost immediately" means in
the hoverable next fourteen seconds.

Services such as HBO[67] and Pay-Per-View through those services and a program-selectable format of ATSC anticipated broadly.

We see, as film libraries grow, most people who are willing to give a movie an honest viewing are seeking to enjoy the film, more than own the film. The few exceptions are the movies so adored by cinephiles they demand the extra features and add the Versatile Disc to their personal or professional repertoire.[68] We, with children, also recognize the appetite of children is insatiable and Hollywood only caters a few films a year to their audience, despite massive revenue. We see box office for most films last for at most months, normally weeks, with classics, at least in Los Angeles and other cities, re-viewable at historic theatres. There is demand for the ATSC Streaming on-demand format, and we are a uniquely approved propaganda movement.

In the late sixties and seventies, technology manufactures sought rights to films for sole-consignees for the upcoming VHS/Beta war which the studios were anticipating. Home Movie viewing was going to be increasingly affordable, and ironically enough a huge profit-maker. We saw this again in

---

[67] Who we would still happily take money from. After all, the film is already made.

[68] Rarely, both.

high-definition when HDDVD and Blu-Ray duked it out. Would the fighting have been as fierce if there wasn't a revenue stream? Probably not.

SAG, the Screen Actor's Guild, set a goal similar to my own in Cinema-Libre. They, as a goal, wanted to be concerned with how often the movie was seen and how well. Jack Palance, then the president of SAG, spoke at my College Convocation for my Bachelor's Degree, and challenged our generation. He expressed our generation may not be able to predict where our money comes from considering how his generation in the field DVD was never imagined at the time of filming for the majority of his films.

In the Cinema-Libre, we bypass distributors in favor of this option on actual delivery of content. Are we trying to not get paid? No. But what we're trying to do is frontload payment once the film is complete. Box office makes money, Physical disks make money, Posters make money, physical soundtracks make money, airing makes money, but from there lets keep movies cinema-hyphen-free.

I propose we increase digital libraries and encourage box office and rampant sales when the DVD first comes out to be primary, with strong secondary from cable and streaming for income and continuance, and the pantheon of the library being allowed to join great books considered an element of our shared legacy. We intend to release all cinema–libre films[69] to at least sixteen screens in theatres nationwide in the United States, and we enjoy state support. As a result all of the films we make are theatrical quality. Although such a goal may show cost, money does not exist. I feel as filmmakers, if we aim for pantheon acceptance, our quality and care will increase, as will our product–goal of our films being films of our time and above our time. Our goals can be unadulterated so as a result, ingenuity can be crafted. Craftsmanship is a derivation of function and goal. In Economics, Ingenuity occurs when Goals are multiplied by Goals, written as $Goals^2$.

Propaganda often takes on the goal of expression of morality and unity and as writers of faith and belief proliferate, so too may their messages that are adoptable by people beyond their religion and upbringing.

Understanding religion as an aggregate to be a positive thing, as believers of religion and society, writers of faith have a necessary effort to proselytize beneficial beliefs and knowledge for betterment of society as a whole, without turning away their audience. Otherwise, how else can they

---

[69] Including documentaries.

be received? With morality and interest intertwining, the system becomes more palatable, solitary, and sound.

When I set out to write this book, I had a specific goal. This book will help you to understand Propaganda, the Zeitgeist, and how to use writing tools known as Ideation Tools, although much of that effort is now in the Handbook for writing for the movement. Through the enmingling of the course to the book, the reader will also learn how to set goals and measures to guide the projects to success.

Anyone may participate. I believe, if a teenager has an idea worth listening to, if they champion and foster their idea, they can change the world. Likewise, the same opportunity exists for other traditionally downtrodden people such as women and people of minority. I would love if, for example, a woman offers me a script she loves, even if she is the type of writer who has been working on "her screenplay" and only gives me the one, and I am able to then make a film men love also, at the time of making the movie.

I have the same acceptance goal for minorities, same for youth, and same for nations where they have not traditionally penetrated beyond their own boundaries in their mainstream cinema. I believe we, as a company, can make this type of film again and again, each one being new and totally different.

I learned, "Structure Frees You," while I was in film school from a professor we nicknamed "Fast Eddie" DiLorenzo, as he often maneuvered his class with sleight-of-hand. He taught us the rarity with which a young artist invents something new. What he expressed to us is that good writing will often emulate a formula model and if we allow our fiction to enter into something we as human beings realize within ourselves, and as a species have realized before, we will put forward something we as artists and humans really feel.

SUMMARY

Consider we can recognize propaganda and propaganda dissemination, especially the ideologies as expressed in this book, as more important than the imagining of distribution. Morality is key to all media. Depiction and portrayal, when well designed are intentional. I'd encourage you further in your joining strive. Go beyond simple profit goal and into manifest effort. If your goal is to be a filmmaker, be a filmmaker; put your movie on the wall. If you use my tenets, boil them slyly down to 1) Don't be downtrodden. 2) Be Inspired. 3) Buy my DVD and enjoy behind-the-scenes special features when we're at distribution.

If writing, while you are writing, know that most likely nothing will get you closer to success than completion. Even if your half-finished screenplay were purchased, it would no longer be yours to develop freely and would therefore feel like less your creation. Be diligent when you can and complete your goals.

If you are writing screenplays for example, expect your finished product to be about 110 pages, 136 scenes and at least fifteen characters. If you add a concept a day, you may finish but you might only write one screenplay in your life. At the very beginning of the writing process, however, if you add a major concept a day at the early stages you will eventually be pleased with the progress. These little seedlings will eventually grow to be your project and each seedling line will add to the overall complexity and beauty of the story you eventually present. In other words, you will feel you have told the story you intended to tell.

Gently re-focusing your thoughts is almost always of long-term value. Ideas may come when you are writing other ideas. If the concept seems like a whole new project, give the ideas their due and get them into a new binder and a new set of tools. You can always move them later.

One of the best pieces of advice I got about writing concepts and screenplays during film school was, "This is your time to have ideas. You can develop them at the point in life for the development of them." Provided diligence in clearing them, a project journal for every project is of tremendous benefit and may help you to span into whole new endeavors beyond your goals, by spanning into whole new physical junctures.

Quality is a difficult thing for you, yourself to assess as estimating quality before the words become semblant can be difficult. Frank taught me, "There is a fineline between cutting a corner and bending a rule." Even more elegant, he taught me there is more than one way to bend a rule and more than one way to cut a corner. He for example, taught me to cut with a brush, an expert technique that applies paint exactly and eliminates the need for guide tape.

Help others to succeed. Allow the people around you success as one step to being surrounded by successful people. In Hollywood, sometimes people get jealous. Hurting bottom line option for his employer or studio is guaranteed to make a guy "can-able" also know as fireable. "Cannibal" is sometimes used to describe behavior in the industry as the business is so ruthless, they will rip into the material which had kept the guy there, if owned by the employer they have helped the other lose. Material is principal, and at best well-invested in if even with time, effort and attention.

Consider your presentation. If your project feels wordy, you perhaps haven't molded the wording the way a potter shapes clay. Often, people struggle with whether their product meets the quality they want and judge themselves harshly. Others are unrealistic about their quality compared to an unseen market.

If you aren't writing, are you content? Can you practice yourself? Do you seek a career as a writer and can you set down ideas long enough for them to grow real to you? Yearning and longing aren't the same as doing. David Mamet gives phenomenal advice on this in his book *True and False: Heresy and Common Sense for the Actor.*

Writing, the actual art of putting words on a page, can feel choresome. Ideation, a major part of writing, almost never feels like a chore. The ideation tools should make a writer able to enjoy ideation with no more labor than moving a pencil or a pen and persistently thinking.

Using an author of a book as an example, his or her first goal may be to complete the book. A second may be quality or to feel the book is the book the author feels is his or her own. A more advanced writer may add that they didn't want the labor to feel overly laborious. A more prolific writer may feel the success is setting goals for yourself from which you aren't willing to deviate.

Writing, filmmaking, playwriting, composing, all of them have the same phenomenon. You get out of things what you put in, and for a writer this includes time and exertion. Are you safe enough to forget your ideas? Are they well enough recorded they are also safe if you set them aside? Value contentment and be strong enough to take the time to rest. Relish rest when rest comes.

For the Littérateur, writing tools that are clean and prepared, as well as predictable, are obvious assets in forming the ideas to words before they are forgotten like a dream. Clean and prepared, the ideas are held to wakefulness.

If you would prefer to be writing and feel discontent, consider your tools. Have you cleared all of your journals? Have you re-explored your character cards? Have you read the proper books of inspiration and have you surrounded yourself with things that remind you of your goals and progress in mindful ways?

Do you feel you need to show someone your work or have your progress validated? Consider the characters in the world of your story. Find people like them in at least setting and find how they feel. Remember you need their permission to depict them. Most people are enthusiastic.

If the world was a monkey and the monkey wants the best six years of his life, making movies is fun. Being a filmmaker is fun. Editors are filmmakers. Writers may be, although I agree with the Writer's Guild of America statement, "Writers wrote those words." A distributor isn't a filmmaker. At distribution, the film is made.

Good advice is often not profound. If profound, good advice has profundity due to simplicity. Expand in your story what is simple and universal. Enjoy the process of writing at the least and continue to move the pen. Frank used to express, "Finish Finesse," or ending the job well, as the highest ideal in professional finishing.

When asked what a contractor is, Frank would say, "A contractor makes a contract." Everyone wanted to be the contractor. What they wanted was the power, and those men often weren't the rightful wielders. They were less looking at what they would give, and more looking at what they would get. A life lesson is to offer more than you seek, especially opportunity.

Learn to use your tools to the fullest. The pages of a notebook are like a carpenter's nails. At first, the carpenter feels of his nails they are a commodity to use and leave behind. He cuts wood and assembles his structure. Eventually, the carpenter reaches a level of respect for his own work where he would like to leave the nails he hammered in place.

I am Master Horseman. I am also Self-employed. I am the Founder, President and Visionary of Vision Quest Entertainment Incorporated. I indisputably have a job, but since the founding of my company in 2003, I have needed a second job from time to time. I won, in a drawing lottery, professional software for word processing.[70] This win started me on a path towards what you are now reading.

I function as my company, Vision Quest Entertainment Incorporated. The goals of Vision Quest Entertainment Incorporated are making media through profession and trade. We incorporate the rules, as stated in this publication, as the rules of the Global Film Movement, The Cinema-Libre Film Movement. I am proud to say I am an open propagandist. Not only do I announce my cinema and the rules to apply; I also allow others to submit. Like most in my business, I do not accept unsolicited submissions, but my rules are posted and announced.[v]

As a director, I am fairly well-known on set for saying as a mantra: "Make my shot, make my day and make my movie." This book is designed with a similar utilitarianism in mind, but I have endeavored to not force this book to be "Make

---

[70] The software, while tremendously useful, made me slightly more prone to the famous Adobe Virus. I extra-hate the Sun Microsystem drives the virus is on.

my story." Instead, this book is designed to say to make from what you feel, a feeling story. This book, in the series, is designed to help you to write a story that is native to you, but to help you to feel freer through the use of my tools, including my self–imposed rules.

As the author, you can endeavor your own way. What inspires you, write. Things you have seen and things you have experienced can be made to be drama for you. Put the drama on the screen. Use your project journals and keep your prized ideas as sacred and included in the mix. Go over them often, and especially, put your effort towards your goals.

ENDNOTE ACKNOWLEDGMENTS

[i] A Riesling monkey is an intelligent animal. I was one time "rescued" by a Riesling monkey who like to spend the day up in a tree with her daughter. They defended their banana grove from bugs and intruders. If they didn't', the bugs would lay eggs in the bananas and whole crops would have been lost. She was an expert at rock throwing and from her tree was able to hit a flying jungle bug, which is about the size of a human hand, from about thirty feet away, even if they were moving. The Rieslings eat the bugs and she was fairly wealthy in the amount of fresh bug she spread around her tribe. Her daughter was hyper-intelligent for her age, perhaps from the hours spent

with her mother in the tree watching and listening to the humans. On one occasion a bug flew at me as the instructor was explaining the day to me, and then flew about four feet away at hover. She hit the bug, I looked up at the tree, startled, and she smiled and laughed at me, proud of her shot.   When she took her eyes off of the bug, six other Rieslings, endangered species at the time, came out to take their piece of the carcass. She was disappointed to miss out on the bug, but glad I wasn't angry with her. She and I, and later when I gained more of her trust, her daughter, became good friends.

The monkeys love to spy on humans. In Panama, when I was in field training, the monkeys would even breach the secrecy of their espionage to tell stories and even tell jokes about what they had seen. They laugh like horses, with a chatter and a nod.   Rieslings and horses also believe in God and can pray.

The Rieslings are a very clean species and bath daily. They give gifts of apples, which they polish like a human woman would wrap a gift. They barter for bananas, which, if they are the trader of, they break open with a fist to make the banana only good for a little while, a tendency we call "punch a banana."

They explained to me, a husband raises the child until he is two years old (an adult in their culture). For a polygamist husband, he has two know the wives as individuals, they explained, "this one is this one, that one is that one." They admitted their husband had, before, become angry enough to punch them indiscriminately. For each of the wives, the wife only has sex with the husband and bathes him daily.

I recognize the behavior of the other primates as natural and moral. I believe I have rights of enactment of natural and moral things, even killing. I learned a lot from these little monkeys, and they took the time to explain to me a lot of their morality. They demonstrated their mating habits and marriage rituals, especially one monkey who was two and a half and her husbands other wife. They are polygamist, and I believe they have a morality which is well worth the comparison study to our own. The thoughts they as a collective share as to what is right and wrong, what is allowed and what is morally offensive are an example in the animal kingdom of a zeitgeist. I don't agree with their policy of felatio-for-bugs, which they eat, and a few others, but I know I feel this way and they feel they are Rieslings.

151

Since they are not burdened by language, their rules are quite simple and easy to understand. If people can know the rules, the rules are much easier to follow. I am pleased they have shared their culture with me. I enjoy their friendship.

The Riesling Monkeys grow to sexual maturity at the age of two, and are white-haired by seven. They, as an example, have a decade of human life equivalent, every year. As a result, their families are as though a four-year-old is raising a child. The father has a responsibility to raise each child until they are two and can take their place in the tree defending the grove. From there on out, they have earned their keep to their society and eventually, like our own servicemen often do, can retire and raise a family.

One of the monkeys, an adolescent female who considered herself pretty, attempted to share a skit with me. The adolescent monkey with a younger male showed a skit where she put her face in her paws and had the other monkey lay on her back (actually rolling like a Chinese acrobat onto her). He explained, he was a monkey in a tree and she was a tree, with a monkey watching. They were letting me know, more than one of them had been spying on me when I was receiving my training.

152

The same monkey found me a few days later. She had practiced a skit with one of the women in the Army. She approached me and signaled with her paws for my attention. She asked me to speak what she gestured. She pointed at me, and I said "I." she moved her hands at her own mouth mocking human speech to a crowd, "Tell everyone." She signaled to the suns path showing many days and shrugged "Eventually" she pointed to the Earth and showed a big ball with her arms, clearly rehearsed, "If the World" and then she gestured to herself, "Was a monkey." She nodded, believing herself understood.

She came back later to clarify, she meant I tell people "If the world was her." I still use the phrase, often, "If the world was a monkey." She felt I can keep using the phrase, so long as I believe we are both being the same kidded. We weren't mean-teasing, a very important concept to the Rieslings. She wasn't stupid and I valued her attempt at communication. As long as she and I are the same made fun, she had accomplished the goal of her skit. She and I are friends, and I am still happy to remember my friends.

In my first few days in the jungle, one of the male monkeys, who had a young son, befriended me He performed a little skit which suggested once he was young, now he was older, and soon he would be a dead. He would then with a comedic look on his face suggest we could give him banana chips (Baked slices of banana which were dehydrated). He had been storing them in a tree, getting ready for retirement. He had two wives as the monkeys allow polygamy. They bath their husbands every day. This is a measure of a wife, along with their "gesturing out of their lady parts" he is the only one to have their kid.

   The family let me also meet their son, about the size of two fists, and I admit I felt very privileged to get to have hugging level contact with him. His son was rapidly learning the jungle, still wild animals, and his knowledge growth was very real to my training as many of the same things a danger to him, would have been a danger to me. The son is well-noted to have practiced climbing on me. The father taught me the very sacred-to-them method of softening a banana to feed an infant, and admitted he knnew I will be a good father come my time to be a dad. One of his wives, the one with the new puppy, believed him. The other thought he was simply telling stories for banana chips, which are banana slices baked in an oven.

   One of the Rangers I was training with was diabetic, rare for the army. He tested his blood and the monkey went well beyond spying and announced, he is learning and also in the grove. Whereas I was still just a kid, the monkey trusted me. The monkey took interest in the test as the ranger squenched his face, not needing any problem on the issue.[71] The Monkey shrieked and made clear, he wanted to know his own. He also wanted to know why he wouldn't die from the jungle and infection since "paws touch dirty" and to the monkey standard he would be wounded to the point of blood. We explained to him the alcohol swab, and we showed him the pinching of the swab in the testing fingers. We were also curious about his blood sugar. I tested mine for him. He saw the process and then volunteered, already scared about his health and already self-limiting his diet.

As the machine calculated his result, he stood there, waist high to us, pinching his alcohol swab in his paw like a human does. We realized we didn't have any idea what their blood sugar is supposed to be. His younger wife and son volunteered for the same test. They were both at a much lower level than a human would have been with comfort. With simple comparison, we found him to have much higher blood sugar than his son and wife.

---

[71] His blood-test was also a slightly higher read than he would have preferred.

Considering how such information can be devastating to humans, the monkey actually stayed very brave. He refused to believe he was in more danger than before, and he was already self-diagnosed. No shock to him, he now at least had Tremendous{The Ranger} and me believing him. He also had already shown signs of depression. He gestured to Tremedous. The monkey asked me why the Tremendous isn't scared. I explained to the monkey, we had a treatment structure. He wanted to know if he could, too. He, within ethics, volunteered for the undertaking, so he walked with me onto the army base {much to their surprise as many had never seen a wild Riesling Before} and we got him to a vet to experiment with medicines. The vet found the monkey was diabetic, no doubt. The vet showed courtesy-care and the tone of voice now made the monkey very sad and he realized, he had seen other monkeys die this way. The monkey knew we had not done this on monkeys before, but accepted imminent insulin treatment and later in the week, metformin, a drug that accelerates blood sugar reduction. We were still doing on why the drug worked at the time, and the monkey thought the test sounds good.

The data-expectation across species was invaluable. The Army is still doing studies where the monkeys volunteer for testing {often in tremendous pain if they do not have treatment}. The army set written measures for the study. The Monkey, we nicknamed Eddie, pointed to the written measures and explained to the vet {violent Primate} this meant he gets human medicine. He returned to the jungle confidently diagnosed and concerned with his reliance on the humans.

News of the treatment spread amongst the monkeys. One of his wives climbed down from a jungle bush after his diagnosis and gestured to me, "Do you know what guy I am?" Somewhat similar to horses, the female monkeys sometimes don't acknowledge gender. I knew what she meant.

The monkey's young wife was about two, barely past adolescence. Her husband's family was obviously affected by the diagnosis. She was nervous. She gestured, pointing to the ground with both hands to me in a very common for their species method, "Can I sit?" Which in behavior, basically asks if she is safe to share space with a human. I assured her she is safe with me. She knew if I let her sit with me, she is allowed to be nervous. She began gesturing animatedly, indicating and reminding me of her husband's skit where he would show he is dying and would like a banana chip. She reminded me, in the skit, her husband is dying. She reiterated, her husband is talking about dying and his blood sugar is confirmed. He isn't really dying she asserted with a small screech. I explained to her, "Humans take blood sugar very seriously."

"Why isn't he scared like me?" She pantomimed.

I explained with a shrug, "His diagnosis is confirmed and now he knows what he was feeling is real."

The word "Real" was enough. She, in response to my statement, shook her head, "No," another common behavior for them. She refused to process and resisted believing.

I reassured her, "Also, he knows the humans know what to do for the humans at least."

"She gestured with me with one finger defiantly to herself and me, "That was what she wanted." Her husband ended up volunteering for sonogram and insulin testing, and the pharmaceutical companies lined up for testing opportunity on a species far closer to human than rats or mice, and clearly volunteering within ethics. She was very, very much calmed. He later volunteered for X-Rays also (knowing them at least to me, more dangerous than the drugs) in exchange for seeing the results of his X-rays and other tests and us having a greater knowledge of his live anatomy {he understood this useful}.

His other wife, the one who had doubted him, made a point of finding me later. "How'd you calm her so much?" She asked of the other wife. I could see she was sad. She looked left and right and gestured, "Can *I* sit down?" I was very calm since the army had already given me clear. I indicated yes, and, sinc eI knew the girl had been a little mean to her husband about his fears, looked to her softly inquiring with my look, "Is she self-aware and is she OK?" She shunk up a little nervously and suggested I had gently scolded her with my look and as to his health, she admitted with a head nod, she had been in denial. She looked to me quizzically, also wanting calming.

I explained, humans are studying her husband because we also have this high blood sugar. After the response from human medicine for their veterinary treatment, I stated for the first time with reality and permission from the Army supporting me as the measure, "We can keep him alive. He hasn't died from this."

She indicated I had given my word, stating her own measure of what I had said to the depth of her love for her husband. She believed me, but wouldn't tolerate lying.

I added, "He still needs to show up for treatment." She said she would make him. We agreed. He showed up to me again, with real emotion. He explained at the opportunity, "For as long as he is a monkey, I have a friend who is a monkey."

As measure, the Army found he showed up every day, as regular as baths, which the wives give their husbands everyday. He died years later of what the monkeys and some natives call, "Bones," or Leukemia. We studied him all of his life forward and he died a white-haired monkey, as he had wanted.

I was called by the army with the news of his death, as his son (who I have known since he was a puppy and is also a very good friend for life of mine) had requested. I received the call while at an Anthropology exhibit. His son shared his feeling with the mourning. The monkeys believe I had kept my promise unsullied, his father had not died of diabetes. His wife had kept her promise also; he had shown up for treatment.

The big breakthrough for me in terms of personal goals of advancing medicine with the opportunity and not seeing monkeys in pain at the level the boy scouts taught me to send a human to the doctor finally came when Department understood the studies are not on caged monkeys, but on volunteer wild monkeys. "Why would they show up?" they asked. I pointed out, our problem in the human world, especially in gerontology at the time, was no one really wanted to go to the doctor. Department streamlined the application process for the pharmaceutical companies and made clear to them, if the treatment wasn't "Ouchless" and "Fun" enough, the study failure was their fault. I added, the monkeys are already in tremendous pain for many things and completely untreated. "Ouchless" can be "Ouch-Less." The pharmaceutical companies again lined up. So did the monkeys. Eddie's bravery and his success had encouraged them . They did understand we were studying them. A few insisted on meeting a human who wanted the same thing done to him or her.

[ii] A Monkey I knew wanted to marry. He had opportunity with a girl he liked enough he felt he would accept her as a wife. Her father had said yes. He believed this would mean she would bath him and have sex with him. To the monkey standard, the younger monkey had not yet learned (indicating with hands) this one is this one, this one is this one, which means his wife is unique and belongs to him. The girl monkeys had made sure I understand this because they want me to marry more than

one girl. The monkey was young enough he was still learning about sex. He showed a pattern of aggression the older and younger monkeys did not. He was at the age, he didn't recognize his own aggression. He simply thought he was unique. I learned from a friend who has some-expertise in both dogs and horses "Learning about dogs teaches a little about horses and learning about horses teaches you a lot about life." Watching him take husband responsibilities, I learned a huge amount about both their grove and his growing family.

The Rieslings have a tendency to base their behavior on a human, similar to little kids playing make-believe. One of the monkeys had begun to base himself on an Adjutant General I know well, who goes by the moniker "The Little General." The monkey wanted to learn how people make things. He understood humans have things, but how? He also took the opportunity to admit he like the example of macaroons, inexpensive cookies the army in the field would sometimes trade to the monkey for raw goods like coconuts. I still trust those little monkeys to pick out produce for me, which they polish and present with pride like we wrap a birthday present and a card.

I got permission from base to bring the interested monkey into the kitchen area, a very rare thing, but the girl who was running the mess promised Department of Defense she would clean the place before and after. She wanted to meet a Riesling.

He walked with me on base and was patient when I went through the protocol coming in from where the field rangers were training me to the more domestic areas of the base. He and I got into the kitchen area and he immediately marveled at the stainless steel counter. He understood humans use the counter to make things. For him, at least, his question was answered.

He went back out to the jungle and tried to explain to the other monkeys what he had learned. He found a flat rock made of flagstone which one of the other monkeys believed he owned. He tried to set the rock on some other rocks and the other monkeys all laughed at him. "That isn't how humans make things." They clearly believed.

He was dejected. Some shrieking occurred and he wanted me to explain to them. There was eventually some squabbling amongst them and the girl wanted to meet more Rieslings. She allowed them in to see her make macaroons. To the Rieslings, a species who doesn't even like fire, the oven was a fairly impressive thing. They went into a frenzy when they could smell the macaroons cooking so close to them, but they weren't ready to be served. Again, the Army girl cleaned the mess to human readiness.

[iii] I am enthusiastic about recent changes in law, notably the now demonstrable ability of the president to fire judges. We have learned from school house rock and Social Studies, The Executive Branch check the Judicial. Now they may.

The federal government has long been emboldened by the claimless self-hype of the federal troops. I would love if the Stolen Valor Act would take us to the complete opposite extreme of what was common when I grew up, of sons of marines waving their father's devices in people's faces and them claiming themselves threatening. I would love to see all of the hype from the Federal set be only what is real, and none of what is false.

We shall go farther. I know the Federal Government claims congress has the right to fund agencies, such as the DEA, but I know the reality is our founding fathers left undeclared rights to the states in the tenth amendment, final amendment in the Original Bill of Rights. I believe in State's rights and am proud of recent advances in states overcoming federal in both marriage law and drug enforcement.

I find many things about myself bettered by the buddhist concepts of right thought, right goals, right actions, right mindfulness, etcetera. I do find these things cross over beyond portrayal and into the real world. I, myself, am staunchly heterosexual. If anything, my derivations bend towards traditional polygamy, where I am the husband to multiple wives. I have had many girls, worldwide, express strong interest. Think harem girls and Jacob's wives more than something new and risqué, but imagine each of the girls gets her own room. I think my thoughts worth expressing on the subject considering the states are now letting gays marry. I, again re-iterate, I am not gay. I have no interest in sharing my wives and I have already lethally defended my own.

I dislike and deride prostitution. I believe men who have to pay for sex are uncharming enough to covet women beyond their charm and their lethal appeal, and uncaring to hire them if hiding behind secrecy. I do like the girls, though I don't pay them. I do also note Christ spent time amongst them.

Men who find themselves generous for paying are hiding their lust baseness behind false grandeur. I can, however, believe as I have used the Rieslings as example, there are plenty of examples of when a monkey would

165

trade what he has for what he wants. If the world was a monkey, would you ever give what you have for what you want? Yes. The difference on the monkees and the trees though, is they believe their community owns the yield of their crops. Our human system uses money which is a far more efficient commodity. I dislike the lack of distinguishment.

As I contemplate portrayal and display of sexuality, I think back to early human, before the invention of the prophylactic. I care about how they kept their relationships strong, I believe both man and woman benefit from intimacy in the relationship. Not all sex is procreative. Even species beyond our own enjoy joyful copulation, felatio and raunchy storytelling within their own cultures.   The felatio allows them the inspection of each others genitals, intimacy, and an outlet which allows them to plan pregnancy and child-raising.

[iv] An example of what I do as a Military Anthropologist is to sometimes bridge gaps on understanding.   An example is a conversation with a daughter a General from the Nation of India, rightfully perceived romantic by her, involving understanding of their peoples' point of view on Health. She made a comment about American "Being Fat" talking of how such hurts the organs. She agreed

{her English being solid} the medical term "Obesity" made sense to describe what she had said, at my prompting to the escalation out of loose-language and into medical precision. I shared, we, in America, in medicine have made great growth in considering Obesity a disease, similar to Alcoholism, beyond the simple thought of the person is "fat" definable by body shape. She felt when she looked at me, similar to financial terms, she saw "The Gross of the Guy." She wanted to "net" me. I had lost my training wheels on this on several daughters of the Navy and Air Force. For her feelings, there was not such a difference between "fatso" and obesity. She is very svelte, and she has goals for her own health and family. I appreciate her. I thanked her for the medical appreciation as well, and showed her physical strength. She found me very strong but possibly too heavy for physical health, which she valued over physical strength. She reminded me, the medical caste in her country had been rejected on the issue in 1973. She returned to what I had offered on Obesity in our modern medical culture and made clear, she liked our new and improved point of view better.

India spread the word of our exchange to all traditional cultures. One of the big things about training is if they met a soldier they can now express their enhanced point of view. They felt vindicated as their cultures felt, "we said, we said" regarding the issues of body fat and organ health. Now, the medical condition "Obesity" meant "the medical condition characterized by Body Fat" which again meant their culture felt "We Said, We Said." when before Western Medicine had formally discredited them. They were unyielding in their belief and eventually western medicine caught up to them. We had simply never bothered to tell them, they are proven correct. They were grateful for our contact.

India is a nuclear power. In the interest of our military, I not only gained a fresh entrance to their body of knowledge and belief, I also assuaged standing anger in their society towards the west. I also gained a friend and asset on a personal level, who still helps American interests at my request. One of the nicest things about Army Seduction is you can accomplish your objectives and the target of value is still alive, still friendly and still intimate, ready for contact.

ᵛ In regards to my business and operation, I am hostile and defensive. This is the third company I have founded and the realest. The first two, founded in Oklahoma, Left of Center Productions and Right of Passage, were both attempted at hostile takeover by purported Billionaire Harvey Weinstein, whom I despise. He attempted to buy them for one dollar, and disallowed the founders into court. Left of Center had three corporate officers, none of us was allowed to speak at the hearing. I knew he would try again when I founded Vision Quest Entertainment Incorporated in California. Weinstein is the second target objective for Black Rook, in large part due to his purporatations of funding for support of the now removed due to corruption group of judges, Richard and Richard Rico. He has often supported them when they have had to go beyond their then more-official abilities to defend their Racketeering Involved Corrupt Organization. They, in turn, have let him steal intellectual material and held people who would argue against him out of the courtroom.

I designed the company as bait for him, while at the same time tried to build the company asset by asset. My first five months in business we made enough to purchase our own editing system (now defunct, save software) and we started our first year paying taxes, a mark in California the company is a success. He tried again to buy the company, again disallowing me into the courtroom. My accountant testified and we defeated him. He claimed he had spent tens of thousands on legal… we found he had used that exact legal on four other companies. He had still only offered me a dollar. My fight was a success and the company has now won the right of Federal Protection.

WORKS REFERENCED:

A Chorus Line: music by Marvin Hamlisch, lyrics by Edward Kleban and a book by James Kirkwood, Jr. and Nicholas Dante

Writer's Guide to the Hero's Journey: A Handbook for Screenwriting in the Cinema-Libre Film Movement, Alexander Valdez, Vision Quest Entertainment Incorporated, 2012

Spiral Dynamics. Cowan and Beck.

Screenwriter's Notebook: A Remedial Step-by-Step Guide to Finishing Your Screenplay, Alexander Valdez, Vision Quest Entertainment Incorporated, 2012

The Visual Story, Second Edition: Creating the Visual Structure of Film, TV and Digital Media. Bruce Block. Focal Press, 2008.

Das Kapital. Karl Marx. 1867-1894.

Psychomachia" or "Battle/Contest of the Soul," Aurelius Prudentius, 410 A.D.

The Masks of God, Vol. 1–4. Joseph Campbell, Penguin Press, 1991

The Power of Myth, Joseph Campbell, author with Bill Moyers, Collaborator. Anchor, 1991

The Artist's Way. Julia Cameron. Tarcher/Putnam Press. 1997,2002

Gunfighter: AGWC (A Gulf War Chronicle), Mark Medoff, Samuel French Press

Contracts for the Film and Television Industry, Mark Litwak. Silman–James Pr; 2nd Expanded edition (February 1, 1999)

Million Dollar Baby: Stories from the Corner. FX Toole. HarperCollinsPublishers, 2000, 2005

The Power of Now. Eckhart Tolle, New World Library, 1999

Civil Disobedience. Henry David Thoreau, 1849.

The Art of Happiness, Dalai Lama, YEAR

I Ching: Or Book of Harmony, AUTHOR YEAR

True and False: Heresy and Common Sense for the Actor.
David Mamet, Vintage Books, 1999

Copyright Basics, United States Copyright Office,
http://www.copyright.gov/help/faq/faq-protect.html

http://en.wikipedia.org/wiki/Maslow%27s_hierarchy_of_n
eeds

http://en.wikipedia.org/wiki/Direct_cinema

http://en.wikipedia.org/wiki/Jean_Rouch

http://en.wikipedia.org/wiki/Kino-Pravda

http://en.wikipedia.org/wiki/Spiral_Dynamics

About the Author and the Book

Alexander Valdez, acknowledged for feature film and network television, has received a Bachelor's Degree in the Fine Art of Drama and a Master's Degree in the Fine Art of Cinema-Television Production. He is a National Merit Scholar and the President and Visionary for Vision Quest Entertainment Incorporated. He is also the author of *A Writer's Guide to the Hero's Journey: A Handbook for Screenwriting for The Cinema-Libre Film Movement*.

The Author says of himself:

I am Master Horseman of the Fifth Cavalry of the United States of America. Master Horseman is a Position Posting, not a rank, but I do have excellent standing and training, field and class, and also over one-hundred clear kills (C.K)., most against armed men who meant to interfere with Operation Black Rook and meant to hurt or kill me.

To maximize their investment in the soldier, the Army gives Primary, Secondary, etc. all the way to Tertiary to all counted assets. Primary is what you do when called to that level of duty, Tertiary is what you do most. My Primary is Master Horseman of the Cavalry, My Tertiary is Spec Ops. Prep, including barber, uniform, uniform-detail, logistics, battlefield surveyance, wordings, measure and goal. I have not acknowledged rank.

My predecessor, while teaching me, as far back as pre-teen, used Basketball as an analogy during the famous season of Duke University's "Dream Team" which included Chrsitian Laetner, Kobi Bryant and a very Young Shaquille O'Neal. After their NCAA win, they left to "make the money" in the NBA. Several boys were in attendance to the call. For their and my benefit, my predecessor compared the Army and the National Guard. If the players consider themselves, "Basketball," the Dream Team of Duke were also upgrading to better coaches and better coaching by going pro, something which can benefit them for life.

With this knowledge, he left me to my own with these concepts in mind, to develop important legal, with expert Master Teachers from all Branches, including the guard, and with legal support. Theobolt often had a dry sense of humor, and, quoting the First President George Washington, referred to how many of his guys did something insistently inappropriately enough, they don't fear double-jeopardy. "On the Actions, they are clear."

In the cavalry, we still use ancient legal. We also, at rare times, have to defend our own. Theobolt used a still questionable technique in Vietnam called non-rout. The goal was to keep the enemy fighting, at risk. The old horsebound legal on-rout was to disband their unit with force and make them run away. If they are running, we are allowed to pursue, which the Fifth did ruthlessly and personally.

We were surprised when the Vietnamese complained about our tactic. One of the main issues we had used repeatedly was regarding their kill of a soldier we believed had a duty officer. The Vietnamese complained we had not announced which horseman in our Cavalry had a duty officer. If they attack a horseman with a duty officer without killing the duty officer first, we can retaliate with precision and lethal vengeance. I have a duty officer, so I know this legal very well. If they killed one of ours who is so protected, we may counter until we feel made whole. Their complaint, at war, was not our ability to assign such to any officer we choose. Their complaint was they were not told which soldier had such right. I have upheld their complaint. I have also upheld our verbal and military reaction-response. I have had to do this often, very rarely bolstering or renewing the sentence.

He left the Vietcong the legal need to keep fighting. The technique is similar to an NBA player jumping from the three point line to shoot a scoring basket, but intentionally landing in the two point area to send the game to overtime, to exhaust and further risk them, in, for example playoffs. This was before Hearts and Minds.

I have apprenticed several times in my life. My first time apprenticing was under an Amish Candleman. I got to be his apprentice for the day and loved the gentle warmth of the room and smell of beeswax. A superbly beautiful girl, seven at the time, she thought, also enjoyed the below-earth depth he used for candlemaking and she found reason to spy on him and me as I was learning. Her family owns the book-bindery in town, and they had fresh butched a cow when I visited. We ate well that day.

In the brief amount of time I spent apprenticing under an Amish Candleman as a child, he sent me out to explore the village a little. I was urged to help the beer and wineman who was trying to clear a well-set root from his field. The root had dug deeply and he had weakened the root through hard labor, cutting away at the tendrils which were holding to the earth and cutting towards the root-stump itself. He had his animal, a horse, set to the goal. The horse was pulling but couldn't understand how the enterprise was going to yield the root pulled. I stood to the horse, the beer and wineman tended to the pull and harness.

I vocally encouraged the horse to not give up. He pulled earnestly, his footing loose in the plowed field but his trust in the humans earnest. He looked at me with an incredulous look on his face, securing he was doing the right thing to keep pulling. I encouraged him again and lo, the root came free. Everything in life that requires straightforward effort is a little like pulling with blind faith in the exertion to see the root-stump come free.

The Candleman's shop was unbelievably tranquil. He used burning wick fed by tallow under the pot which burned at the temperature of the molten tallow in the pot.

Calmly, not disturbing the tallow, dipping wick over and over again until his candle reached a size he know he can sell. He explained to me the concept of Master Workman and apprentice: You can learn what I do, but you do the work I tell you.

Very soon after, I met the first Master of Apprentices where his apprentices would not hesitate to call him master. "He is the Japanese Paperman" I learned from his two female apprentices. They make paper in the ancient way. When asked, "Why are you THE paperman of Japan?" he would respond, "Want to buy paper?" In the scant weeks I spent around the girls and later him in a class for gifted and talented, I learned a lot about paper and also Japan.

I later apprenticed under a more modern man.
Contractor R. Frank Barnes was noted for mischief.
When "FineLine" Frank was feeling mischievous, he would
talk. Frank was the master contractor for the whole
operation and everyone wanted a piece of what he knew. I
was one of his apprentices, and have grown to filmmaker
and for my own company, security contractor. I am now
noted to be able to be in charge, especially with security
contracts and with security apprentices, including highly
lucrative. I've learned the goal is always stop-loss and always
for the contractor, contract and deliver the contract.

People asked Frank, "Where did you learn contracting?"
"Contracting." He would reply with a small smile. He
answered several questions the same way. He was a master
teacher. He expressed to his apprentices the benefits of
learning, especially if there was also a little bit of money
around at the same time.

As Frank used to say, "A safe workspace is a clean
workspace." Frank himself balked at saying a clean
workspace is always a safe workspace.

Frank would fire on a safety reason so fast, if someone was
drunk or meandering, we on site, sober and focused,
expected a firing if we saw someone out of the safe range.

The last thing Frank needed was a lawsuit and the first thing Frank wanted was profit.

In the painting business I learned, most guys who do this for a living are normally happy to take the job so long as they don't have to lose money in the long run. An example in painting would be uncovering damage, which your insurance would need to cover, or anything else, which would uncover a second repair such as a wall exposed to elements or insects. In contracting, similar to a mechanic, a contractor has to at least be able to return a site to the previous condition. Sometimes, this was impossible as before a master contractor got there, the site was unsafe.

Frank had explained so many things to so many people, he admitted, sometimes he didn't bother to teach the basics. If he explained something at the level of knowledge of Master Painter, we could later ask the painters or master apprentices, "Is that what Frank meant?"

I was distinguished amongst the painters for asking well, "Am I doing this right?" They noted if the job was clean and prep, I was cleaning and prepping. They often had a better way. They had had my job before.

For you, as you encounter endeavor, if you find no one around to ask, "Am I doing this right?" I would recommend to you to return to your goals, look at the larger agenda and simplify your efforts.

A Frank statement I still regard highly is, "In a perfect world, a perfect man would probably get everything right." He didn't let his apprentices slide on complaints of a task being too difficult. He offered promotion and profit on excellent demeanor. He also denied work on drinking, on the site, for personal safety issues. Frank had certain limits. He'd normally self-impose them.

Frank Barnes was a United States Marine in the U.S.M.C. He commented, "Lethal killing is insipid with tools." He killed at seventeen. He saw 'Nam, he fought in post-Korea. He was there when the Army killed the emperor.

Every once in a while, Frank had a way of saying the word, "Paint." He would soften the "t" to suggest pain. "For a master painter, pain(t) is applied. For a well-oiled team, no one spills pain(t). Spilling pain(t) causes disruption, and causing disruption causes dis(may)." He suggested with this last wording, painters might not have work next summer. In painting, firing an apprentice comes easily. Frank told me, "The reason I'd fire an apprentice on the spot was because of a safety issue. The reason I'd fire a man in my office was to settle the client or to make the man feel the right way." He smiled at the word, "man" knowing he had come of age. He said of his apprentices, "On some days quantity matters, but most days quality matters most." Quality counts.

Frank worked in excellent woods. I recall, one time we were working in aged mahogany, bought by the gross, which the lumberyard delivered as 4"x4". The gross was less expensive than the size we needed, 3"x3".

"This is a terrible waste of lumber." The master carpenter said as he ran piece after piece through the lathe, cutting the 4"x4" into the 3"xFix. Frank pointed out, at least the lumber was used.

Frank's normal job was ten days long, often luxury homes or apartment complexes. He normally had work planned for the next eight months. Frank taught me that in the field of exterior painting the job is half about diligence and half about neglect. Our part is the diligence, and the neglect is what we came to remedy.

Again, using painting as an example, when you first show up, the whole thing is needing to be explained. We get things done by explaining them as we do them. This lasts one time each. Questions? Ask the foreman. This isn't shop class. He know his job, your job, that guy's job. Do the labor and don't get fired. Hollywood is even less generous. No one will teach you unless they get paid.

In painting, eventually, someone may show up newer than you and get taught around you. After all, you get paid together. You repeat step one, getting things done as they are being explained. Eventually you come to realize, the guy is talking, you know the job. The site may be different. You adjust. You eventually know how to adjust.

I had discussed some interest in eventually making movies, a job which does require contractors. Speaking as security, the well-respected talent often gets protection. Even the protection is sometimes protectable. I was eventually teased for my interest in making movies, and was sometimes derided. Welcome to the worksite where my friends who were fired before me named Matt and Nick were referred to as "Gnat and Mick." Firing for drinking was one of the most common as safety on the site is everyone's job. The Master Painters knew the job and the craft, while Frank had the clients booked until the end of the season and next. All in all, I found more effort than failure, and more endeavor.

Frank taught me to respect the master painters know more than I do about painting, and the master painters don't have to do the somewhat monotonous job of prep and labor I had as an apprentice. Genuine Respect for those men and what they gave me generously as long as I gave them me, back. As an apprentice, someone other than me sets the task. Getting the work done is the job and the apprentice is responsible for the general safety and prep of the structure. I still, at times, find myself preparing the structure. I thank them for their giving. I found the men eventually came to support me. I offer you a similar flavor of support, and again, I thank you for your giving.

Beauty and love amidst war have encouraged my growth as a Filmmaker. In the events of 9/11, I was set to active in Operation Swift Response, the immediate planning and debenture of all troops and units directly under President George W. Bush. I was the guy in charge and also the declarer for Afghanistan. I was at the University of Southern California at the time and one of the Lady Trojans on the Soccer Team, Star-Stryker for several seasons, Jacquelyn Onassis (Granddaughter of the famous Jacquelyn Kennedy-Onassis for whom she is named) is Muslim and Arabic Fluent and was there at the same time I was.

With a position at captain readied-by-Bush and the nation at highest call, I said in response to there queery regarding would I transition from black operation to open service "Where and When" giving them permission to let

185

me know where I would be most effective. I responded
with affirmation for them to simply inform me, which they
failed to do, but at least this time notified me of their failure.
I went in to the recruiting office and they claimed they
could only give me the first initial of the base to report to,
later found to be Fort Irwin in California. They also
purported they even had cab ready to take me there, but
again the corrupt on admitted fear kept me uninformed.[72]

Upon further complaint by me, and at request for service,
the army got me only unofficial as to where to respond.[73] I
had a similar failing from the military when they were at
specific-from-the-President before when my predecessor
passed away in 1996. I was eighteen at the time and young
for the job, but needed. I was requested to Fort Sumpter, in
Illinois, for enlistment by Forty-Second President, William
Jefferson Clinton III, himself. A daughter of a Marine, Kelly
Pingle, got me the message, and I am proud of her. I'd let
her be my love-slave.

---

[72] The corrupt judges also had staff there who eventually threatened a horse I love, not my duty-officer, named Cyborg. Their files weren't even accurate enough to find past equinity.

[73] I found out later, Bush had formal waiting for me and had even provided transportation at least beyond my own '69 Karmann-Ghia.

President Clinton had asked the men at Fort Sumpter to "Sign him up." I left within the boundary of time Clinton had set. After a disagreement at an Illinois toll-booth, I was given Police-Escort by Highway Patrol. With four squad cars leading me, the base was notified of my approach. Their adjunct, a member of their secret group known as talon, called Rico to find out what to do. They had prepared her for the "duty." She denied her colonel the information the President had called. She claimed, when questioned why she hadn't relayed message, "Her Colonel is an important person"

I approached gate with an allowed-for-me procedure and they opened bar. I was fired at on base-grounds from the tower, which was under direct-order. They sent dogs out to meet me, barking ferociously, which I recognized as unbriefed and tamed. I withstood the bullet-and-dog assault, still on my feet. I asked why they hadn't heeded presidential advisement. The Adjunct announced, she thought her Colonel was important. Their general admitted ineptitude. I discharged his weapon.

I was already being quoted in the press at my position. I had to defend the state-of-the-art Apache Class when Congress was claiming them obsolete. Congress had refused part-and-pieces legal for them, at their own failing. The

American people rallied behind my efforts considering the enormous cost already sunk and the quality of the gunship. They agreed we should have these gunships up-and-flying.

Back to 2003, The state department and military abandoned me at USC without a comm system[74] with Jacquelyn and a female journalism student, both Muslim and Arabic fluent when the United States of America could barely read and write Arabic. I am trained to seduction and measure. Both were useful towards improved communication, which the Pentagon felt was worth more than a simple-field-placement of me. I am trained to Apache Gunship and would have preferred more fight. I assisted in logistics and tally-measure of swift response via telephonic for that whole six weeks and as an open propagandist, was also led to graduate. The General of the Second Division of the United States Army actually came out to campus to congratulate me on graduation and upheld my education as of value to the Army. He also offered some legal support. On Conduct, The General of the Army also attended campus to thank me the semester of my graduation with my first Master of Fine Arts. With his support, I again

---

[74] State was afraid Advanced Communique would be discovered and my position as formulative leader anticably threatened.

re-iterate I'd of preferred more fight and I don't feel I was well upheld at non-standard tribunal to issue regarding uniforming and command. I regret their poor recordsmanship, and I do point out, I had been afforded a Judge Advocate General and Non-Standard Uniform Tribunal, but was put to Standard Uniform Tribunal without a JAG.

Under Clinton, I had been afforded a JAG, presumed to be an honor. She was signed by Clinton to make sure "We don't have a problem because of Alexander Valdez." She actually then flew out to felate the Ricos (the Corrupt judges who are primary target of Black Rook) and they suggested reasoning on her violating all terms of her service. She complied to their request instead of Clinton's. At my tribunal (which I had not been notified of), she failed to show and didn't even notify me of the hearing. I am not sad she has died of heart Failure at Szabo's restaurant in Oregon. At the time of the tribunal, I was still in film school and in close-to-weekly contact with department and executive. They also failed to notify me.

My division is voluntary reserve. I was set to academic for my active-structure.[75] I have still not seen pay. I have,

---

[75] Active-Academic

however, been taught "A Patriot is someone who stand with his nation when they need him the most." I reported for my classroom training in the next calendar year, Formal at the Armory at the Univesity of Oklahoma.

I am still in service and I will most likely receive Black Barring on my service tally. Still though, at the massive "Highest-Call" I was already on the phone with the president and should have been moved to open service. Why didn't I at least have my Jag? The army has since cleared me of abscond (Still under Bush) and upheld my film school training as propagandically important (I do hope this book is self-explanatory), but I still hate the black bars on my sleeve. I was in Black Rook the whole time. The five/sixths of Marines who did nothing but train and waste money best not punk-lock on me. I outset them and outnumber them single-handedly on kills[76], and I think they have nothing to show for their time and expense. I note to them, the men you so poorly trained lost Mosul in three days. Yes, I can blame you.

If I know one thing about policies and protocols, it is that if you stay within them you have done so. If they consistently use the term "Punch and Wallop" they

---

[76] At least those I have compared to and who have made public their selfish gratitude.

consistently mean the term, "Punch and Wallop." I was given broad protocols with specific policy. I was and am granted General Operation within written parameters of Operation Black Rook, a discoverable Black Op. Op Blk Rk was written after the freedom of information act, and is a discoverable black op signed by Clinton.

At call, under Bush, they missed my legal and wronged me greatly. At Uniform Call, I may wear their shame on my sleeves. If your device misses this, I rec. you report. I am active-operation on operation Black Rook, and will remain so until achieving total success on operation parameters. During operation, I have over fifty self-defense kills mostly from corrupt police who are former marines, most of them non-enlisted. I really look forward to opening the record with an official accounting written by someone other than me, expected at the tail of Obama's Second Term Administration[77].

Meanwhile, I maintain the primary, secondary, and third target objective as well as the goal(s) of Black Rook. I do have some legal support and am treated to the legal at the level of support. The Operation has legal support in defense of democracy, signed by 42nd President of the United

---

[77] Right before Administration Clearing.

States, William J. Clinton III. With expertise, I expect total win. I feel, in doing so, I help America and the World. Confused? I encourage you to activate your rights under the Freedom of Information Act.

Much of what the Army trained me on in Battlefield Opportunity can be boiled down to a feeling like ten-year old boys fighting after school. Example:
"I'll fight you, but if you kick you're a cheater." Says the first boy."

Option-Response:
"I don't have to kick to beat you."

Optional-Option Response:
"If you can't handle my kicks, you're a pussy."

Either way, whether option-response or option-option, we would most likely not fight unless kicks were agreed to or ruled out. In this example, the side aggressive to the fight wanted no kicks.

Another good and useful example of modern war and fielding is as though we play chess, but we agree we aren't using bishops and we each only get one knight.

I am trained in getting the enemy to the battlefield. I invented Asymetrical-Symetrical Warfare, Transponder-Responders and the immutable physics used in the zone part of Crumple Zones, which the military uses daily in Non–Crumple Response.

I am the son of an infantryman who made cryptographic specialist. I am sure you have heard of the 82nd Airborne Division. My father was advanced infantry in the 82nd. I was flagged for the Cavalry by the age of ten. Much of my training was unofficial and started well before eighteen. A Ranger showing–up to check on me was not an odd thing in my childhood. Later, they developed the early–unofficial to official–official. I have excelled in foreign–field training[78] and I thrive to my expertises. I have also excelled and am able to train classroom.

On Black Op., I can separate to Official Army. I was signed by Clinton as "Army of One." I am trained in full–scale, even less than total. I am one of the army soldiers called off after Hurricane Katrina. The Cavalry was authorized to fly four–hundred Chinook helicopters, gassed and manned and ready to go, when the state department called us off claiming class B emergency. There are more than rumors, they were motivated to deny us glory.

---

[78] light-heavy

In the Navy, glory is their motivation. I respect the genuine Navy SEALs. As for others, I don't need unexploited warriors, especially if they have only trained on pay, telling me their thing. I would rather have a kid tell me a Karate Story from after school. As for famous, skilled and intelligent men and their exploits: ideators, innovators, inventors and imagineers; they may share with me. I prefer NASA to most servicemen, again, especially if they have never seen beyond training.

The Navy mantra Valor, Honor, Glory evidences. Can Faery tales stay out of war? Our recent flinging of Navy Seals at the beaches of West Africa caused obvious and needless loses. They are using pre-Normandie techniques trying to emulate success from the Raids of Osama Bin Laden, which they did not plan causing losses.

My Cavalry is the cavalry who took the Seals into Pakistan to Capture/Kill Osama Bin Laden. They were under my planning and direction at the time, including discovery of the location. On the same mission, my Cavalry is also the Cavalry who brought them back after we had to send our own reserve craft after the helicopter crash blamed on "Hot Weather." I also ordered the return to Standard Operation Procedure, which resulted in the Burial-at-Sea of Usama.

The Marines might have found Saddam Hussein, but we got Osama. I also note, the Iraqis had no weapons of mass destruction and nothing more to do with the attacks of infamy than you or me.

A man once said to me, "War and Killing are basically the same thing." He supported war in defense, but was not yet lethal.

I responded to him, "There are rules in war. In killing, there is basically 'The guy isn't alive anymore.' The Boy Scouts would say, 'No pulse, no breath, no brain activity.'" I feel well trained, and ready for open-instatement.

I was granted light-rouse right as a child by Forty-First President of the United States, George Herbert Walker Bush, whom I consider a patriot. His son helped me out a lot of the legal for this book, without delay. I thank all of his sons and especially granddaughter Barbara for their support on the project.

I was granted light rouse so early as to allow my thought process to adapt to my special legal. I didn't grow up on base, and I am famous within old culture for explaining to kids my age, "You aren't in the army on the base, you are in the base on the Army." The sentence is multiply interpretable, part of standard army wording.

Light Rouse is similar to kid magician, where you expect the kid to pull out flowers. I, as a child, was the Amazing Alexander and I am noted to have invented the Shuffle-Ruffle and the Ruffle-Shuffle for card tricks. One ReAstounds if the trick went awry, the Other is magic, forming a heart with the card lay. I found my efforts of practice as a kid magician did a lot for me later in everything military, from wording policy to hand-to-hand exchanges[79] with procurement as a goal.

The Army often has a forward and back-peddle-able written style, which they esteem highly. I am trained to be an expert in Army-Wording policy. The Light-Rouse construct was instrumental and thought process I value and enjoy, and think fast.

I believe rousal, at best, is light. I still believe the Childhood adage, "Secrets, Secrets are no fun. Secret Secrets hurt someone." I wish people calm. I have full-divulgence with privilege.

I feel and I know killing with supremacy is moral and just or not supreme. Depictions of killing should always allow

---

[79] The FBI keeps files on every lethal soldier. I am, according to the FBI logs, what would be considered a connoisseur collector. I have dated more than one girl at a time and I didn't have to lie to any of them. The CIA taught me there is intel and agents. Put them together and you have something close to intelligence.

for the moral and emotional underlay, with sensitivity for the trial of human life. Heal the world with your violence. Anger, jealousies, all are violent. All are "you want to change the world from what it is." If you are going to be violent, help society. Not everyone who is violent is a killer. A traditional saying I learned in my Prussian fencing education is, "If you want to kill someone in a society, find a man with a sword and have him help you." Obviously, this works even if you have your own sword. Violence is violent, killing is final. We normally have found things beyond threat, which can further us. Love is more beautiful than violence and should be depicted as such. Violence is Quick and Ugly. Depiction of violence should be functionally immediate, and may be ruthless and direct. Seduction is beautiful and lengthy. Love may be languid and sincere.

I've chosen to live my life as a life of faith. I am a Christian, a Buddhist, A Daoist and a Sikh, without conflict. I do have a Sufi Muslim name, Muhsin Annour. I am deeply religious and I allow a religious morality to guide me. I am receptive to other seekers, regardless of spiritual path, so long as their morality is lucid and open. I believe God speaks to us all the time but difficult to hold, and, like deep suggestion, his message is worth remembering and therefore, worth writing. I believe God Self-Published the Universe and at times makes gentle revisions.

Prayer is not always secret, and not always sacred. When God speaks, best he is remembered, as, like a vespers, his voice is sometimes soft like a child's voice and divine, whether Alla, Allah, God, YHWH, Yahweh, or Jehovah.

I have learned for myself to have faith and set my own purpose. I nod to this gently and unadvertently in the structure of my first tenet in the Cinema-Libre. I endeavor, while challenged in the market, to make something in my creator's image, and to make something my team and I are proud to show to the world. I have learned to keep a journal. For those of you who had not set to write, consider, if well urged, to at least set pen to my feelings.

I had a general one time tell me, there isn't anyone exceptional he is aware of who hasn't had this stuff given to him as kid. I had a lot of people from the army check up on me, especially in elementary schools.[80] One of the things I learned, especially from female officers who hated they were up against healthy and naive 19-year old-girls fresh out of basic on the "check them out for duty" scale taught me about the importance of experienced staff. "They are important, others are important also."

---

[80] Sometimes comically after playground fights, sometimes with children of other army measure.

Can a private be important? What if he or she was sent to relay to a senator? What if they are nervous? They are important. Yes, private is important. I have had this hammered into me since childhood. The Attitude eventually can express beyond rank and into simple human understanding (where rank still factors, due to chain of information and command). The thinking becomes super easy to do and super easy to remember. Respect they are there.

I have enjoyed training in the field. In addition to field training, much of my training for the Army occurred in a college environment. I learned all information can be put into a file, a category, and a cross-referenceable. My training was "Classified means Discernable." As such, all information, as an expert, is classified. Classified may mean sensitive. Classified may also mean protected. Classified may also mean ready-able and _____. (The latter there is open to if someone working with me has a different working wording. Each student is given at least two of these.) Highly Classified means it is specific. Add in concepts of "Need to know" such as division, pay grade, rank or other measures and now the system of classified information is as you know.

We were offered Reserve Officer Training Curriculum. The Acronym is discernibly R.O.T.C. As such, we were given classified R.O.T.C. training, and discernibly so, I am an expert in "Why We Fight." I was given a leg-up on eventually studying to the War College standard, military Anthropology. The classes were also deemed appropriate for conscientious level students, including potential objectors, whom I may teach. What would they do? They offer and learn "why the objection?" while I know "why we fight." I am trained to believe them, patiently. I know, sometimes our best propaganda comes from overcoming objections from our brightest minds.

With Military anthropology, we study cultures' concepts of God and the Devil, Good and Evil, Pre-historic patent, etc. Their concept of history was different before global. Instead of simple fame, they wanted to keep their things. An example in keeping tactic, every kill, pre-acknowledged and planned, had a trick or rouse or a new technology. Why else show off? I learned in Karate as a very young child, "Fighting isn't fair."

Part of my anthropology expertise is advanced morality with advanced sexuality in the military. I endeavor to demonstrate morality with advanced expectation of respect. I am allowed to bring up subject with a very diverse group of experts and I am regarded by them as both an individual and Army of One.

My beliefs often excel beyond other people. I believe in Holistic medicine. We have a remedy for everything wrong, even if that remedy is under six-feet of dirt. As I mentioned in the Forward, I am barber on Spec Ops. Prep. An example of the holistic medicine I believe is the Minoxidil Root, commonly sold in America under the trade name Rogaine. The stuff is powerful and natural, and the pygmies do use the drug also to announce Cancer. They believe the minoxidil to be a sacred plant.

Another example for me is Marijuana.[81] I believe the protest chant, without hurting Joe SixPack, "Man made Beer and God Made Pot. Beer is legal, Pot is What?" Growing more legal.[82] I have tried almost all of the drugs I mention in this book with Marijuana, which I have also used medicinally. I was taught by a native shaman as a child, "If you trust a plant, let the plant be your guide." I do note, my friends the Cherokee taught me they used to look for

---

[81] I am aware the DEA has claimed a heavily refuted study since the sixties. I know the Army and those involved did a secret counter-study which is FIA-able and their study was radically refutory.

[82] I note that while congress has the right to fund agencies, they do not have the right to violate Amendment 10, which should have left all later funded agencies to the states.

tobacco. If they found other plants in their search, even better. An example for me of responsible marijuana medicinal use, which I have enjoyed as a tea, focused on the clippings and trimmings. Rapid, racing thoughts are diminished and the thought process is much more content and enjoyed.

I come from an ancient family. We have more than one way to spell our family name, as our family is very old. One spelling is Valdes, which suggests "You Evolve." Another, perhaps more ancient is Baldés, which states "You Blade." We are known to be descendants of the swordsmiths of the King of Spain. When my name is written in Spanish, we use the appropriate. I have a similar in the Arabic Language.   In Arabic, my name is written as Muhsin Annour when, for example a movie poster would give credit to me in their language. Muhsin Annour means "He who is engrossed in good, The Light." I am proud of my Muslim name. I try to live up to the naming. I know as an artist, I am healthier if I know myself, even if vulnerable.

I am the twelfth Guru of Sikhism, endorsed by the building of a Gurugranth Sahiv for me. A main tenet of my religion, which incorporates other religions, is "Are they rational and reasonable?" A friend of mine once asked me, in belief, what of reincarnation? I responded, "God is believed omnipotent. This would mean, God can do anything. I believe part of his omnipotence may be practice. Reincarnation fits in." My predecessor at the Fifth Cavalry Stated, "God doesn't have a perfect plan, that's why he needs us.

The many who believe I am the Sikh to be the Twelfth Guru, believe the cosmos was created for such a person, but he is still just a guy. The Tenth Guru stated doubt in God, regarding the arrival of the prophesied Guru. I was taught God is omnipotent. The Vatican also believes me and It's Religions to be the prophesied acolyte of Martin Luther.

I have found in the effort to have diverse religions incorporated me into their enclave and for me to include their beliefs with my own, I normally need to relax dogma and embrace sincerity. One of the reasons I love Los Angeles is the network of religions that co-exist there. I feel welcome, at least on the inner fringes, of all of them. All of the Christian, Buddhist, Muslim and Sikh have gone beyond fringe and into welcome. All of the religions above have offered me food and friendship, and sometimes coffee and discourse. I am less an oddity to them, and more a scholar.

My Monk-Friend and Professor of the Buddhists, Dr. Suthiyani Phramachanya shared with me some of his learning when he was getting his PH.D in Comparative

Theology. He shared about religious ceremony and theory, I am welcome if earnest, and earnest if sincere. He is an excellent monk, and taught me much of my meditation knowledge.

For people interested in religions beyond their own upbringing, I would suggest the same lesson of sincerity. Approach openly, and with kind regard. I remind you, again, they are religious about their religion. Respect their upbringing is key to their understanding, and you have not been raised in their zeitgeist. Expect to learn more than teach. Expect to listen more than talk. Expect to use "you" more often than "I" and hopefully you grow to use "we."

Be Well, and know they aren't necessarily looking to share their religion with someone who would water their own down. I had an opportunity on the Isle of Crete to pay homage, through my own risk, to their statue of Poseidon. Their midwife had shown me around the island, including showing me Cretian numbers which state to the times in their history, they have built things such as cannon foundary for defense or other foundation. I was eventually shown where their secret statue is, off the island wall and in the sea. I, while a Warrior of Crete was warning me of the dangers of the ocean, stripped down to what I learned in swimming merit badge and cannonballed into the sea {I had been promised legend of exploit if I made actual contact with the statue}. I swam down to the statue, embraced him, and then returned to the surface for air. I, thin at the time, lifted my out.

"How did you pull yourself out?" He asked me.

I began to explain the method I had been taught when I heard from the far end of the Island, "Shark! Shark in the water."

I looked at my male Instructor of the Isle. I had contemplated the danger of Ocean Currents, but figured others had swum out. I hadn't contemplated sharks.

The tigershark swum over and gave me a knowing look, clearly still smelling my presence. I gave a slight smile, knowing I had already met my side of the deal of exploit. Now the deal was sweetened with a shark.

The man of Crete, still, appreciated my bravery, when fear may have been unknown to me. I still consider them friends.

Many SEALS are of a Crecian Bloodline. They set me to real standard for them as a warrior, when I was taught a mentality of having a "Weapon and a Knife." SOG briefly made a knife[83] for me in honor of the exploit called the

---

[83] Technically the word in Ancient Crecian translates to Sword-Thing.

"Tigershark." The thought process is a common one which makes any future exploits better teaching tools for their younger warriors. The Crecians have a word which is all one word for "Better Stories Told." The word is not allowed in Athens.

Many of the men of Crete are actually an ancient religion[84], all the way back to the rowing mariners and "they actually found their way. If you can meet one, let him tell his stories, no matter how ancient or far-away.

I have invented dozens of inventions in daily use by most people. I invented transponder-responders which eventually took us from Walkie-Talkies to cellphones. They are also in use in fax machines and modems. I invented post-integer calculus and am the first person to change a law in physics, notably the law of aerodynamics. I also proposed four more which have all been upheld. I invented paladential thrust and lift, which is in use on the F-22 forward.

I invented pay-in-play videogames, an invention I was supposed to be paid 50% of all total revenue. I have not yet seen a single payment for this invention, although Glu, Firaxis and Deadman's Cross have said they will pay.

---

[84] As are many of the Greeks who have stayed close to where, from their point of view, "Our ancestors did something."

I invented the zone part of crumple zones for an inventors fair and invented immutable physics as a result. I am still owed $500 for every vehicle which uses the technology and as of the date of this publication, have not yet seen dime one.

I am the first to solve the Socratic theorem, although the initial fanfare was stolen by Johnnie Rico (Son of those corrupt judges), who didn't even know the basics of my proof. I am still furious.

I invented Perpetual economics, first out of hatred for the corruption which Black Rook fights, in which I show the corruption and theft of efficiency causes us to lose growth when we should be building on infrastructure from before and also should be "Pure-Gain"[85] on natural items such as crops and Green Power. I designed Perpetual economics to at least show a mathematical model for a world without corrupt judges, NSA, etc., who are neither worth secrecy not power they are allotted wrongfully and shamefully. Governments have begun to implement the theory and are showing great result.

---

[85] Pure Gain Model of Perpetual economics does include macro growth from new equipment, machines, and infrastucures such as irrigation, land-lay, and foster.

I presented to the state department what they called "The point of view of a genius child." What they were working with was an undeviatable policy of No-Yield on nations who were holding POWs. I was granted light-rouse as a child when I sought to offer a partial clemency to nations who had POWS within their borders regarding at least the knowledge of where the Prisoners were being held. An ancestor of mine as a famous quote[86] regarding "What's right and what's reasoned." The state department hadn't looked at their process for years and no a single POW had been released.

I spoke to Vietnam, first. A future friend and training officer of mine, Brian Drake, had had one of his training officers captured when he had tried to break some known captives out. The captured officer had perhaps seen Rambo a few too many times, and he didn't know the held captives would have rigamortis from lack of exercise in their holding. I met him years later in Colorado after his release, happy to see him. The Bush administration hoped, since he was a fresh captive, we might have more wiggle-room. I at least got them to promise they would release as many as Korea.

---

[86] The original quote is in Spanish.

I spoke to Korea, next. They loved the clemency deal, and wondered "How are you so powerful?" I admitted, as instructed, the deal is only for a limited time. I also told them, well beyond state department's advisement, of my deal with Vietnam regarding the Korean number. I heard Kim Jong Il laugh in the background. "Release 68," he said in Korean, doubting the power of the Vietnamese.

The Vietnamese scrambled at the number. Who would have believed the Koreans and their candor? Kim did, especially with any clemency on the table at all.

Germany heard of the offer, and a then very young empress offered their four remaining (one of whom was a general and Father of my own Father's former colonel, and grandfather of the current General of the 2nd Division, My Infantry Guard). Germany admitted the men were aging and didn't want to be maligned for any death of them, natural or otherwise. We were ecstatic to receive them and I still uphold Germany's now-current right to a military which for them began around the change in the millenium.

Bush had granted me the power of light-rouse to give me a chance to offer, even if I needed help from a government who might have retreated again to a no-yield policy. The state department bet against me. A then young Donald Rumsfeld, who proved loyal to the corrupt judges who hated me, bet a gold star against every released POW. I am owed 140. The same Donald Rumsfeld, while Secretary of State under George W. Bush later held off on my Cavalry, at my orders, sending 400 helicopters we had gassed and manned and ready to go at the disaster of Hurricane Katrina, in 2005. He reportedly didn't want me to get "Any Glory." Over 1,000 deaths resulted. I helped one captain to fly in the face of their grounding and they saved four and spotted dozens more in the disaster. You do the math as to my four hundred helicopters authorized. During all of their speeches and the later departure of the National Guard Ground Units, my authorization stayed in place. I feel we could have saved all of the victims. I still blame Rumsfeld–and–cohorts for the deaths on a scale of larger than a thousand humans dead.

The Author says of the book:

I spent a semester mentor–teaching at–risk kids remedial filmmaking at Venice High School in Los Angeles Unified School District while I was getting my Master's Degree in the Fine Art of Cinema–Television Production at the University of Southern California. The class was half writing a screenplay and the second half shooting, and editing the footage. Also, the film had "graffiti" publicly made. Many of the students in my group were considered at–risk of graduation from high school. I am proud to say, all of the kids in my section graduated.

We found, as the kids were shy at the first week, and pushed to the limit by the ominous effort of post-production, they wished they had gotten more done in their first three weeks.

I have written the books in the Project Period Series to guide you in your own creating of a well-formed project through a process which will help you to write, shoot and edit your own ideas for a film, streaming media, or teleplay. The series is growing. The series includes Our Story Begins, Screenwriter's Notebook: A Step-by-Step Remedial Guide to Finishing Your Screenplay and A Writer's Guide to the Hero's Journey: A Handbook for Screenwriting in the Cinema-Libre Film Movement.

The successful attacks on the U.S.S. Cole, Attacks on Clinton, and the Attacks of September 11th evidence a now aging call for useful policy. Another, more recent example, The Marines in their tussle, lost their entire F-22 Raptor fleet in one day from indolent defense near-mortar lob, with the obvious sadness none of them had been used for the war, other than target.

The Muslim Talibani and Al-Qaeda, in examination, seemed to no longer slow. Other than the Navy smashing a bottle on a ship and christening their $2.7 Billion overage on an unarmed $30 Billion Dollar boat, the Marines lost more money in a day than any other branch. We note in the military, how many of those Marine F-22's were used in combat: none. I'd like my film movement to be more militarily effective.

The Author says of the book:

   I spent a semester mentor-teaching at-risk kids remedial filmmaking at Venice High School in Los Angeles Unified School District while I was getting my Master's Degree in the Fine Art of Cinema-Television Production at the University of Southern California. The class was half writing a screenplay and the second half shooting, and editing the footage. Also, the film had "graffiti" publicly made. Many of the students in my group were considered at-risk of graduation from high school. I am proud to say, all of the kids in my section graduated.

   We found, as the kids were shy at the first week, and pushed to the limit by the ominous effort of post-production, they wished they had gotten more done in their first three weeks.

   I have written the books in the Project Period Series to guide you in your own creating of a well-formed project off through a process which will help you to write, shoot and edit your own ideas for a film, streaming media, or teleplay. The series is growing. The series includes Our Story Begins, Screenwriter's Notebook: A Step-by-Step Remedial Guide to Finishing Your Screenplay and A Writer's Guide to the Hero's Journey: A Handbook for Screenwriting in the Cinema-Libre Film Movement.

The successful attacks on the U.S.S. Cole, Attacks on Clinton, and the Attacks of September 11th evidence a now aging call for useful policy. Another, more recent example, The Marines in their tussle, lost their entire F-22 Raptor fleet in one day from indolent defense near-mortar lob, with the obvious sadness none of them had been used for the war, other than target.

The Muslim Talibani and Al-Qaeda, in examination, seemed to no longer slow. Other than the Navy smashing a bottle on a ship and christening their $2.7 Billion overage on an unarmed $30 Billion Dollar boat, the Marines lost more money in a day than any other branch. We note in the military, how many of those Marine F-22's were used in combat: none. I'd like my film movement to be more militarily effective.

213

16471135R00127

Made in the USA
San Bernardino, CA
05 November 2014